CRICKET
in the long grass
Village Cricket and aspects of
Rural Life in the 1920's and 30's

Harold C. Woods

Published by Cortney Publications

DEDICATION

To Marjorie
for accepting the role
of cricket widow.

ISBN 0 904378 44 6

Published by
CORTNEY PUBLICATIONS
57 Ashwell Street, Ashwell,
Baldock, Herts SG7 5QT

Cover Design by Jeremy Ruston (Ashwell)
Page preparation by Word Design Technology (Clifton)
Printing and Binding by
Woolnough Bookbinding Ltd. (Irthlingborough)

Contents

List of Illustrations

The paintings, reproduced on the front of the Dust Jacket and in the centre of this book illustrating a typical game of cricket "in the long grass" and that on the back of the Dust Jacket illustrating the posts protecting the "square", and menacing cows, were painted by the author.

Ten cartoons drawn by the author to illustrate various cricket terms are scattered throughout the book. Work out each appropriate caption and check yours against those given on page 96.

About the Author

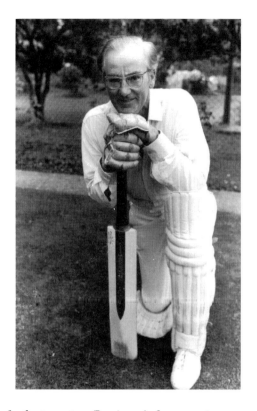

My long and fortunate 'Innings' began in a remote North Hertfordshire village in 1919. A limited education followed, from the age of five, at the tiny local elementary school. At fourteen the big leap from schoolboy to a man's world took place – epitomised by the short trousers being replaced by long bib-and-brace overalls – and rewarded by ten shillings (50p) for a forty- eight hour week.

Cricket was already becoming increasingly important to me, both in the local village skirmishes and through the somewhat scanty news emanating from Lords, Old Trafford or Melbourne. For the remaining years of the 1930's I dabbled in village cricket and was beginning to make progress, when, in the autumn of 1939 I received, from King George VI, a plea for assistance regarding an aggressive and evil character in Germany. Thinking this would take no more than a few months and, that consequently, I would be home again and available for the 1940 Cricket Season, I agreed.

Unfortunately the job took something like five years – after which I was required to help out in the Pacific Ocean where the Japanese had decided to climb on the bandwaggon and take their share of the goodies; this absorbed a further year so, all in all, I was at sea in the Royal Navy for six years and was reintroduced to the cricket bat in 1946.

In 1943, during the course of a 48 hours leave I married my wife Marjorie, the ceremony taking place in Ardeley Parish Church. We had a son, Barrie, in 1947. Having worked pre-war in the Iron Foundry in Cromer for two years, and at Wrights Brewery in Walkern as a maintenance carpenter, which I rejoined after the war in 1946, we moved in 1949 to Stevenage, where I worked in a small business.

In 1956, we moved to Letchworth, and for the next 15 years, I worked at Meredews, the Furniture Manufacturers and then for another 15, at Norton Road School, as a general factotum, cricket coach, caretaker, etc. When we moved to Stevenage in 1949, I joined, somewhat nervously, the Town Cricket Club with its much higher standard of play and grander facilities. This posed a considerable challenge but, with much help and encouragement from the incumbent members, I survived to represent the club for the next forty-four seasons – finally retiring, as a playing member, at the age of seventy-three.

Obviously, for some years before this, I had realised that 'Hanging up my Boots' was an inevitability and some other leisure activity would be needed to help fill the yawning gap the absence of active cricket would leave. Luckily, the desire to be an artist had always lurked somewhere in the background and, as a consequence, this hobby has blossomed and done much to alleviate the loss.

The book I have written is about Village Cricket before 1939 – a very different sport compared to Village Cricket of today, and existing in a village way of life which has essentially disappeared, for good or ill. For various reasons I have used fictitious names of places and people. But readers familiar with rural North Hertfordshire should equate 'Shappley' with Ardeley; 'Clome' with Cromer; 'Cottam' Cottered; 'Barford' with Stevenage; 'Barfordshire' with Hertfordshire and so on.

All statistics given in cricket match descriptions are authentic – having been taken from actual scorebooks of the period.

Preface

Before delving into the problems and delights of village cricket in the 1930's it will be necessary to say something about the way of life, in rural Barfordshire of that time, otherwise the following chapters may be difficult to understand let alone enjoy.

In general men worked a forty-eight hour week, plus various extras, if farming and livestock were involved. Consequently there was little time available for leisure pursuits, especially as the Church required the Sabbath to be completely observed; so a man's domestic responsibilities – such as his large vegetable garden, house repairs, boot repairs, bicycle maintenance, chickens etc. had to be somehow fitted into Saturday afternoon and what evening time may become available.

Cars were virtually non-existent in the rural backwaters and, on the rare occasions that one *did* pass through, the villagers would stand and stare, wondering who it could be – speculating as to where it might be going, whence it came, and why'

There were a few wirelesses around – which required a 'wet' battery for power. Two of these dangerous acid-filled glass containers were needed so that one could be on charge whilst the other was in use; this arrangement called for a weekly cycle trip to the next village where some 'magician' possessed the facilities and know-how to affect the recharging process. Television was, of course, unheard of and, as most people could afford only one newspaper a week, it will be seen that the villagers were very isolated from the rest of the country and the world in general – indeed, the majority had never ventured the thirty miles to London.

It may have been because of this isolation that there was a constant urge to organise, and run, a wide variety of leisure activities to fit the rare days or hours that were available; amongst these was the all-important Cricket Club which, like most things, had to exist on the minimum of members and a constant shortage of cash. In fact, only the benevolence of the squire and his annual 'fivers', dropped into the funds here and there, bridged the gap between solvency and disaster in most of the clubs and functions. The fact that he owned half the Parish and employed some twenty or thirty people at his huge mansion alone may have influenced this largesse to some extent.

May Day at Shappley.

The Village Green.

CHAPTER ONE

Discovery

The casual traveller exploring rural Barfordshire in the 1930's could consider himself fortunate indeed if he stumbled on the village of Shappley. He would probably have stopped his pony-trap – unharnessed the mare and let her graze and roll on the spacious and lush Green – whilst he wandered off on foot for further investigation. Set well away from any main roads or towns the village remained virtually unchanged from one decade to the next. It formed the hub of all Social and cultural activities for the inhabitants of the Parish as a whole, which embraced several small scattered hamlets, all within a distance of three or four miles.

Shappley itself was dominated by a fine twelfth century church looking across the narrow road to the village green – almost encircled by thatched cottages and the matching, all important, village hall. The tiny school sheltered under high elms down a lane nearby, whilst the accepted open-air 'social centre' was an area surrounded by the duck-pond and Blacksmith's shop on one side and on the other by the small shop-cum-post office, rubbing shoulders, somewhat reluctantly, perhaps, with the "Dog and Duck".

Plainly therefore, everybody from all parts of the Parish, found themselves travelling into Shappley, for one reason or another, throughout their whole lives; from christening to burial, through nine years of schooling, church on Sundays, and all social events from Christmas parties to Summer Flower Shows, to Whistdrives and Jumble Sales, Men's club or Mother's Union meetings; plus, of course, cricket and football. Whilst on May-Day every year a maypole appeared from somewhere and the traditional dances were enacted by the very self-conscious school children, in their white smocks and billy-cock hats – watched critically, but happily, by parents who had probably suffered similar embarrassment a generation earlier.

The Bates family lived in a low 'two up and two down' thatched cottage in the hamlet of Clome – near the outskirts of the Parish and a mile and a half from Shappley. As will be seen, the size of the family fluctuated from time to time for various reasons but there would usually be six or seven individuals huddled together in the modest shelter. Of these, young Jim Bates had once again survived a long, hard, winter-enduring, like many other children, frost, snow, and floods on his daily walk to school when such items as raincoats and wellingtons were not available and gloves a luxury for the few. Short trousers for boys was the order of the day and regularly resulted in chapped knees and thighs for several months.

On this April morning, therefore, young Jim was in high spirits as he trudged up 'Clome Hill', with the two buckets and wooden 'hoop', towards the village pump on one of his various daily chores before setting off to school. It should be explained, perhaps that the 'hoop' was, in fact, a square frame made of four, three feet lengths of two-by-one, strengthened at the corners. Its purpose was to ease the problem of carrying back the two full buckets without slopping over into socks and shoes, the technical idea being that, after he'd filled the buckets from the cantankerous pump, they were placed about two feet apart so that, when the frame was laid on top, the two handles were against the outside edge and when Jim stepped inside the square and lifted the whole lot by the handles the buckets were kept well clear of his legs. Unfortunately this did nothing to help his cold hands and only by stopping occasionally and giving them a 'buffet' could they be kept operational. Oddly enough it was in the very severe weather – when the pump itself was frozen up – that he was better off because it then became necessary to boil up a kettle of water to take with him to thaw out the pump, thus he could warm his hands on the hot sooty kettle from time to time on the way up, and, if the pump was in a good enough mood to disgorge its bounty without argument – he may manage to save a little in the kettle for the return journey.

Obviously then, the thoughts of summer on the way were pleasing indeed, for many reasons connected mainly with the elements; nevertheless, there was another much greater reason that brought a whistle from his lips and a spring to his step –

2

only yesterday he had seen brother Jack whitening his cricket boots; *this* is what summer *really* meant! The white clad figures and the 'clock' of ball on bat.

George, the eldest, could possibly claim to be an all-rounder with his bustling, but erratic, fast bowling and occasional runs in the middle order; Jack was undoubtedly an all-round strength to the team – batting in the first four, sometimes as opener, plus an intelligent brand of friendly paced swing bowling which generally warranted a position of first change. Then there was Ralph at the in-between stage, having left school and in long trousers for over a year – but not yet accepted as a player, so in the meantime was involved in the next best thing, by becoming the official scorer for the team.

Young Jim had every intention of following the same apprenticeship if it became at all possible. It may be that this very summer would see Ralph taking his place in the team and leaving a vacancy at the score table – hence Jim's constant buzzing around during home matches last season, helping with this and helping with that and generally trying to get noticed; although, with hopefully, three brothers in the side, his chances for the coveted position must be good – much better surely than any of the other contenders with similar aspirations. Not that the thought of keeping the book afforded Jim any particular joy or anticipation but therein lay the best and surest way of getting hold of a bat out there in the middle, one day, and making runs which was what he wanted more than anything in the world. Why he should have been born with this great urge – or indeed – why all the sons were so keen on sport in general is hard to understand – because Mr Bates senior, not only shunned all physical sport himself, he was actively against it altogether – going, to considerable lengths to prevent his boys taking part until, that is, they left school at fourteen and became wage-earners and his authority in this regard became somewhat under-mined.

Having completed his 'Gunga Din' act for the day and trying to ignore his wet feet, where *some* water had still managed to creep, Jim then picked up his homemade 'Bever' bag, fashioned from the remnants of a worn out shirt and pulled in at the top with a piece of string long enough to hang across his back – thus leaving his hands free for the next job on the list; the bag, by the way, contained his sustenance for the day – usually bread and jam or bread and margarine; to put jam and margarine into one sandwich was much too extravagant for Mrs Bates to contemplate.

Taking their own tin quart milk-can from its hook in the scullery he set off to pick up three more from different houses nearby and headed towards Shappley. After half-a-mile or so he came to a farm standing well back from the narrow country road, a farm which seemed to be forever ankle-deep in mud and swarming with noisy, vicious looking, dogs – although, in truth, these were less of a menace than the huge 'gobblers' that appeared each year during November and December. These fearsome creatures were very frightening, actually making direct assaults on trespassers into the farmyard. The four empty milk cans were left near the door of the dairy and at the end of the school day Jim would find them filled and ready for him to carefully carry back to Clome. This was a 365 days a year chore and brought in eleven pence a week to the strained household budget.

NB: The "Bever" bag referred to above was used to carry the "Bever" or Food snack. This would be eaten during a break from work. Commonly used by farm workers.

GOBBLERS
Some of the vicious feathered enemies.

CHAPTER TWO

School Days

The village school was situated at the end of a lane that seemed always to be muddy – even in high summer; a lane that led to nowhere else but fields, cornstacks and manure heaps – and, apart from the children, was used only by horses and carts hauling their loads of corn or 'dung'.

A single-storey building comprising only two rooms, the school was sturdily built and except for the worst of the winter months, quite a pleasant environment, especially for those children who, like Jim Bates, came from homes that, through lack of heat and light, were forever damp and gloomy.

The long main classroom accommodating about forty pupils ranging from eight to fourteen in age, had ample windows – plus oil-lamps hanging by brass chains from the rafters; these lamps were rarely, if ever, used during normal school hours of nine a.m. to four p.m., but came to life occasionally, with their warm and welcoming glow, when the building was used for some general village purpose on a winter's evening – such as the distribution of free loaves of bread to the very needy every year near Christmas.

Halfway along the side of the big-room was the fireplace, an ordinary domestic type open grate; this was lit at about eight o'clock on winter mornings by Mr Pickering the Headmaster who lived in the attached house. Throughout the school day he attended to the stoking operations and was thus excused for siting his own desk nearer to it than any others!

The importance of this fire, in an otherwise unheated room, gave the Headmaster a useful lever to encourage and foster greater attention and better results from his charges – because those with the best marks and best behaviour were drafted into the front desks nearer the fire – whilst the undesirables found themselves shivering at the back. For those who had walked several miles to school in rain or snow wearing only inadequate clothes and boots this banishment meant a day of physical misery – of sitting in cold wet trousers or skirts hour after hour on hard wooden forms and trying desperately to retain life in equally wet freezing feet by curling up the toes, inside soggy boots, as often as possible.

Apart from this unfortunate aspect – school for young Jim was a most enjoyable time – in fact, he dreaded the school holidays, except, of course, the long summer break which had its own built-in advantages.

The smaller room in this 'home from home' housed the beginners – from five to seven-year olds and was presided over by a lady who, to the very young, would have looked quite natural wearing wings and a halo, despite (or perhaps because of) the fact that she was a middle-aged spinster and was not involved, in any way, with children in her private life. Her handling of terrified five year olds on their first ever day away from home – with no mother available to bring them and smooth over the fearful plunge – was to be remembered by many Shappley folk all through their lives.

In one corner of the boy's dark cloakroom there hovered a cast-iron manual water pump – which, like all its kind, preferred to remain unused and complained loudly and bitterly with agonising moans from its mysterious innards if any boy should have the temerity to depress the handle; indeed, some of the very young looked upon it as something best left alone, and kept well clear of that particular corner; in many cases, of course, it was the first one they'd ever seen because the majority of houses relied on a well for domestic water supplies – these wells were, paradoxically, much more dangerous but less frightening – hence the unwritten law that no children under fourteen were ever allowed near these lethal deep, deep holes in the front or back garden – covered only by a few crooked, rotting boards.

One of Jim's greatest joys of schooldays was the school library – consisting of three wonderful books which he read over and over again; namely, 'Midshipman Easy', 'Robinson Crusoe', and the inevitable 'Black Beauty'; there seemed to be no reading provided specifically for girls apart from the grimy, ink-stained notes passed under desks by the boys.

At the end of the Autumn term each year, a few days before Christmas, the bountiful Squire turned into the muddy lane in his chauffeur-driven Rolls Royce, and, after addressing the assembled schoolchildren in general terms – presented a book to the academic winners of each of the seven standards, plus a bright, brand new shilling for every pupil in the school. Whether or not Mr Pickering received one was never revealed.

The shabby brick-built edifice half-hidden in the shrubbery fifty yards away served, not only the children's basic natural needs, but also in view of its isolation, provided a degree of minor, if unofficial, sex education(!) despite the fact that the building was, of course, built to provide complete segregation.

Discipline was of the highest order, as befitted the way of life in the 1930's; each morning the boys lined up in the playground to be inspected by Mr Pickering, whilst the girls, in their turn were checked over by Miss Endersby, the assistant teacher in the 'Big-Room'. Particular attention being paid to clean shoes or boots – this caused Jim all sorts of problems due to his daily milk-can duties taking him through the ever muddy farmyard on his way to school. Many were the subterfuges and desperate cleaning operations with wet grass that had to be called upon in his attempts to evade the wrath of the headmaster and consequent black marks in his offender's book.

Haytime – a typical rural scene in the 1920's.

7

CHAPTER THREE

Ambition

During that week Jim's excitement grew even more – not only because the first match of the season was due on the coming Saturday – but also because various remarks amongst the older brothers revealed that Ralph would, indeed, be invited to become an official playing member of the team.

With the hope and possibility of moving into the scorer's chair now very real Jim plied Ralph with questions on the subject at every opportunity. Came the great day and, sure enough, whilst he was helping with the various pre-match jobs, Bill Miller, the somewhat taciturn captain, came over – scorebook in hand – and said ...

"Reckon yew can dew the scorin' for us boy"?

Thus the die was cast, as they say, and his foot was on the first rung of the ladder – now it was up to him to consolidate by doing an efficient job. Fortunately, having been forewarned, he was also forearmed – having brought a carefully sharpened two-inch stub of pencil – the remains of a full-length new one, treasured and nurtured as a Christmas present from one of his milk clients. Also he had secreted on his person a segment of an old inner 'bikewheel tube to serve as a rubber – just in case!

During the ensuing weeks, when Saturday was the only day worth bothering about as far as Jim was concerned, he gradually picked up many of the intricacies of keeping the written records competently enough to get by; learning, for instance, how to interpret and acknowledge the intriguing arm signals employed by various umpires; not only did each one do things his own way – which could be confusing enough – but there were constant extraneous arm movements caused by the ever persistent flies; a determined attempt to discourage, or destroy, a vicious intruder noisily investigating the gentleman's right ear, for instance, could easily be construed as a signal for 'One Short'.

Being so close to the action now and listening avidly to the conversation and comments by the players – the lad naturally absorbed a great deal of knowledge about the game and its strange terminology as a whole, not all of which was necessarily advantageous to his future ambitions although he didn't know that at the time!

Such was his eagerness to advance that his daydreams began to see him actually walking out to the middle as one of the team – well aware that it *could* just happen if a particular set of circumstances chose to combine on any one match day. He tried hard not to wish harm on any member of the selected eleven which might cause a last minute emergency for the captain. Nevertheless, such things had happened in the past and could, therefore, happen again. Only last season there had been two such instances when Ralph had been summarily promoted from the scoring position to that of number eleven batsman. The first time involved Charlie Booth – blacksmith and middle-order batsman. As the Shappley players gathered outside the Village Hall, with their bikes at the ready for an away match at Great Sumden, a small breathless girl rushed up to the worried captain with the news – "Dad cam't play terday, 'e woz diggin' 'is fust new 'taters and stuck the fork threw 'is foot". It being already 2.15 by the church clock – and no such things as telephones available to contact a possible replacement – Ralph was automatically 'in'. The second great moment for him was caused by the failure of Phil Todd (Thatcher-cum-opening bat) to turn up; Captain Bill finally gave up muttering and kicking his totally innocent bike tyres – ordered his men to mount up and head for Cottam – their target for the day, with Ralph again becoming temporarily one of the elite. Subsequently, on Sunday morning, it was learned that Phil, this man of many parts, had failed to arrive because his three pigs, two sows and a boar had escaped from their quarters and were gleefully ravishing his spring cabbage – and each other! Such was the pandemonium – considerably enhanced by the screams and highly unhelpful assistance of the five Todd children – that Phil "Clean fergot it woz Sat'dy and that yew uthers woz a-waitin' ". Now it would be Jim's turn to be first in line if any such unexpected events should occur prior to an away match. In the case of a home game there was, of course, more scope for Bill to fill a last minute vacancy – although, in the absence of speedy technical communications, there might still be a considerable time-lag. A runner or cyclist would be sent to this or that possible replacement and if all went well he may arrive at the match by 4 o'clock.

The Village Pond, with the brick-built Well. Reproduced from Hertfordshire Countryside *magazine from an article by G. A. Dunk.*

CHAPTER FOUR

A Summer Saturday

As most of the cricketers worked until noon on Saturdays there was little time available for all that had to be done before the official start of play time of 2.30 p.m. Some, like the Bates brothers for example, lived in the outlying hamlets and may have several miles to bike home from their place of work – have a quick dinner, smarten up, and don the whites – then bike off to the cricket field. The sacred meadow was somewhat tucked away, on part of the Squire's large estate, on the outskirts of Shappley; in fact, it bordered onto the long drive leading to the Manor House itself, so that the magnificent chestnut trees forming the avenue also became one of the boundaries behind the bowler. Like most village cricket fields – its first and primary purpose was to provide a pasture for cattle – and the tiny mown rectangle, cut in there in the middle, would today look as incongruous as a tennis court on the African veldt. Consequently some form of strong protection was required to prevent the cows from meandering all over this tempting patch, which, quite naturally they desired to sample. The fence, therefore, was both high and strong – made of heavy six-foot wooden posts bearing three strands of barbed wire. There were concrete sockets every few yards around the 'table' to accommodate the posts and the whole affair constructed in two 'L' shaped halves – each having about a dozen posts and being joined at diagonal corners with iron screw-bolts; so some ten men were needed to dismantle and drag one half up to the top boundary near the spinney, then drag the other half down to the ditch/boundary at the bottom. It was not unknown for members of the visiting team to lend a hand in this operation – although this might depend, to some extent, on certain umpiring decisions at the last meeting! The fourth direction, opposite the giant chestnuts, enjoyed no natural lines of demarcation, and was therefore deemed unlimited.

Whilst Jim helped with the small secondary fence of chicken wire, (which, in this case, was there to keep rabbits out rather than chickens in) two lesser mortals were despatched to the nearby Lodge-keeper's cottage to borrow the good lady's well scrubbed scullery table and, hopefully, two chairs for the benefit of the scorers. The wooden box of numbers, and the stand for their portrayal, were fished out from under the hollybush which served as changing-room, toolshed, and clothes rack. The club bag arrives – balanced, fore and aft, on the handlebars and seat of Bill Miller's bike. More men appear, in dribs and drabs, from various directions – over stiles, through hedges, and, more circumspectly, on bikes down the road. The visiting team were biking the five miles from Menin and arrived, more or less, together about a quarter to three; some wearing ordinary trousers through fear of getting black chain oil on their precious whites which were rolled up and tied onto the carrier with the usual piece of hairy 'Binder String'. These particular blokes repaired to the uninviting corner behind the hollybush where the necessary change could be affected in some measure of privacy from the highly interested eyes of the various giggling schoolgirls in the vicinity. In the meantime, George and Jack Bates had finished mowing and marking out the creases – pitched the stumps, and returned their equipment back to the all-enveloping holly bush. Eventually, at about three-o'clock, when all the fielders had rolled, and enjoyed their final pre-match 'fag', all is ready for battle – and the two umpires, resplendent in freshly laundered white milking coats, make their stately way out to the middle; whether they walk out together with a friendly chat – or separately in stony silence, again depends on what transpired when the two teams last met.

Having won the toss, Bill decided on first knock so Jack Bates and Fred Owen get padded up as best they can from the sorry-looking five pads available in the bag, here again – binder string, that constant friend and companion of the countryman, is much in evidence where straps and buckles have suffered damage over the years. These two openers can enjoy the privilege of wearing a pad on each leg if they so desire – a luxury obviously denied the rest of the side, unless, it of course, both men are dismissed quickly, in which case some of the more fussy ones may 'double up'. The introduction of that piece of equipment known, strangely, as a 'Box' has not yet reached Barfordshire, so all in all, padding-up is not a very complicated affair.

Jim takes his seat of office at the table and, under the guidance of the captain, fills in the batting order and other relevant details. The order will need to be fairly fluid because Bob Green has had trouble with a scythe during the week and is reduced to wearing a carpet slipper on his damaged left foot, so if he goes to the crease at all it will be as a temporary enforced left-hander. This small hiccup in Bill's plan of campaign is offset, to some extent, by the news that one of the visiting side will be late because he has suffered a "Puncher along be 'Unny Lane" Thus, with the sun beaming *its* approval on the proceedings so far – Charlie who has been shovelling away the worst of the 'pancakes' round the edges of the wicket area, gave it up as a rather pointless exercise and threw his shovel under the bush.

The distant church clock strikes once – "ar parst three then Wal, yearse, jist struck ar parst be the church", observes George to Big Wally-Stanton as they indulge in another leisurely 'roll' and light up.

There is little time for young Jim to daydream about the possible time, in the vague future, when *he* would be one of the white-shirted demi-gods now engaged in battle – because wickets fell at a rate which demanded his full attention to the all-important book and instructing the lesser 'Hobble-De-Hoy', whose duty it is to change the appropriate numbers on the 'Telegraph' board.

The lush long grass, with patches of two-feet high thistles and nettles, in the outfield ensured that only the lofted blow is likely to bring much reward; any stroke played along the ground stopped dead at the edge of the mown 'table' and is rarely likely to produce more than a scampered single. Later in the season, especially during a hot dry, summer, things may improve in this respect, in that the cows would consume more of the dwindling grass faster than it could grow, thus close cropped areas would appear here and there, allowing the ball to bounce and possibly roll.

The Shappley innings follows a fairly normal pattern, with runs keeping just ahead of wickets, at Ten for Six; then comes a flurry of runs from the bat of Alf Marsh who has simplified batting by using a powerful golf-like swing regardless of the line or length of the delivery. To-day he 'strikes oil', so to speak, and clobbers a six and two fours over long-on before missing a straight 'shooter'.

Thirty-three all out is a handsome enough total and will just about allow both sides to speculate on victory during the tea interval.

As the players wander off to the village-hall a quarter of a mile back into Shappley – where tea will have been prepared in typical village style, Jim is faced with the most arduous and only disliked part of the day – for the cows were already advancing menacingly towards that succulent looking, temporarily vacant, rectangle – and armed only with a cricket stump in each hand he races out to begin his hour-long battle with these fifteen four-legged enemies of cricket. Sometimes he received some assistance from one or two other boys who might also be looking for a free jam sandwich brought back by the players, but, today he is fighting alone and dashes madly around in desperate attempts to keep the pitch inviolate; as he bashes one intruder on the nose with his stump two more are stealthily encroaching elsewhere so that he is forced to run and shout continuously to prevent their cruel hooves from injuring the sacred turf.

Suddenly, and for no apparent reason, the enemy seemed to lose interest and withdraw in disorderly manner. With great relief Jim fetches the shovel and sets about removing the worst of the steaming new deposits that had appeared – especially on the bowler's run-ups and the 'keeper's normal territory; there was unmistakable evidence, too, of at least one successful trespasser – at Silly Point, (or Short Mid-On as the case may be), evidence which demands frenzied attention for removal before the men's return – otherwise the lad's protective efficiency may be questioned and his reward accordingly reduced. Fortunately, on this warm July day, the players' stroll back after the interval is somewhat desultory, so he just has time to sprinkle some fairly fresh grass mowings over the offending stains – thus hoping they will escape notice before returning to his seat at the scorer's 'throne'.

Brother George slaps down two slices of well buttered and well jammed new currant bread onto the scoring book then turns his back to lean on the table to roll another 'homemade' in company with his team-mates. Having finished the delicate operation and got 'steam up' once again he suddenly said, 'Ullo, wot we got 'ere then?" and withdraws from his open shirt front one of the delicious triangular iced cakes which were an extra product of the local currant-bread baker.

"I wunder 'ow *that* got there?" says George. "Well blow me if there een't another one?". They musta' cre'p in there summow".

Jim munches quietly away at his second jam sandwich – supplied this time by the Captain, hoping, of course, that he might be in line for an iced cake.

"I carn't eat 'em", announces George, "I've 'ad anuff, anybody warnt 'em afore I give 'em t' the sparrers?". Right behind his broad back young Jim holds his breath, knowing full well that as a mere schoolboy he was not authorised to answer the general question posed by George; in any case, he was beginning to suspect that it was all a hoax perpetuated by his elder brother who had, in fact, carefully nursed these iced delights all the way back from the tea table especially for the young scorer; Jim's suspicions are soon proved right when all the other men vowed they were "Bustin' and couldn't eat no more"; so George, with a broad, grin turns and puts the rather battered looking items onto the scorebook with the words "P'raps the scorer can find a 'ome for 'em, eh Jim?". The Menin scorer had, of course, enjoyed an official tea with the players so all is well for the hard-earned reward to be consumed at leisure.

Subsequently the visitors innings gets underway; their openers prove sound and solid ten runs come without loss and things look black for Shappley – although it must be pointed out that Alf, the main strike bowler, is below par due to his brand new, dark blue, braces which have not, yet 'worked in' and consequently restrict his usual rhythm Fortunately Wally at the other end discovers a patch of daisies and dandelions just short of a length on a line of off-stump and, in the space of three accurate overs, swung the match by reducing the opposition to Nineteen for Seven – and eventually, with the last man being run-out, Menin muster only Twentynine. Several of them are most disgruntled at this dubious end to the game and, without stopping even to change trousers, they climb the fence mount their steeds and speed off with angry shouts of "Yew jist wait 'til yew come over our place, thas'sall". The rest are more philosophical – with one or two even helping to drag the fences back then agreed on a pint and postmortem at the 'Dog and Duck'.

All in all, a fairly typical day and very much to Jim's liking.

CHAPTER FIVE

First Step to Fame

And so our young Jim did his best to keep a clean and efficient scorebook each week always with an eye to the future insofar that keeping on the right side of the Captain was most important – especially in connection with the ever possible last minute vacancy situation.

It was not until August, when harvest-time made its usual inroads into the team, that his great moment came. It was an away match to Netherby, a fairly big village – boasting two pubs as compared to Shappley's one. Ten players, plus umpire and scorer, had gradually collected at the Village-Hall rendezvous on a glorious sunny day just made for cricket. The valuable minutes ticked away and still Tom Green failed to appear, until eventually Captain Bill – looking across at the church clock for the umpteenth time – announced – "Uss nigh on ar' parst, we sh'lefter goo, else we sharn't git there be three o'clock". Then added, for quivering Jim's benefit, "You'll 'efter play boy and we'll mannidge the scorin' best way we can".

Like a Sheriff and his posse they mounted up, with Jim, as usual, balanced uncomfortably on the cross-bar of brother Jack's 'charger', scarcely knowing how to contain the excitement surging through him from top to toe; because of this he became extra fidgety and was reprimanded several times to "Sit still or git orf an' walk". The cavalcade arrived safely at Netherby – but not quite all together, George was half-a-mile behind the rest because it was against his nature ever to hurry – except when bowling. Blacksmith Charlie Booth, number four bat, was even further adrift due to mechanical trouble in that, as he later reported "Me bluddy chain kep cummin' orf".

As Shappley batted first, our hero found himself in his normal role with book and pencil – due to bat, of course, at Number Eleven in the order. Being thus fully occupied helped considerably to keep his nerves and stomach under control for sometime, but when eight wickets were down, Ralph, who had been in and out, came to take over – so the dubious business called 'Padding Up' had to be faced. As there had been no proper cricket or equipment provided at school – this chore was a new experience; with short trousers, stockings, and black school boots it proved extra awkward to fix a pad comfortably onto his thin left leg – especially with fingers that refused to co-operate properly. At that moment of near panic, the ninth Shappley wicket fell – at the healthy total of 52 – and after a quick glance at his tiny number 11 batsman – Captain Bill decided to declare the innings closed. A sad blow for the new, up and coming, 'Walter Hammond', but not totally unexpected, and, anyway, after tea there would still be the thrill of strolling out to the middle with his heroes

The Captain's fielding instructions were short and uncomplicated – "Long stop, both ends lad", he informed Jim; it must be explained here that, owing to the usual thick long grass in the outfield, the long-stop in village cricket was not required to stand back near the boundary behind the wicket-keeper whereby, as in Jim's case, he would need to run like mad at the end of each over to reach his position – no, here the long-stop was really a kind of 'spotter': He stood only some twenty yards behind the 'Keeper and his job, mainly, was to watch closely where the ball landed when it evaded, or bounced over, the 'gloves' or slipfielders whose attention was naturally directed towards the wicket and, consequently, would have no idea which clump of grass or thistles was cunningly concealing the ball, whereas Jim, from his particular vantage point could watch it disappear and immediately shout "I know where it went", and rush to the spot, hoping the ball would not be nesting happily in the middle of a fresh, sloppy cow-pat! So the journey at the end of the over was no real problem. Alf Marsh and 'Big' Wally – the opening bowlers demolished the Netherby batting for a mere Fourteen Runs in Twelve Overs, the former taking Seven Wickets for Six Runs and the latter Three for Three – so there was not a lot for young Jim to get his teeth into at long-stop. Thus, whilst his contribution to the game, and notable victory, had been minimal, his name shone there in the book for all to see:- 'J. Bates. Did Not Bat'. He reckoned his fielding stint to have been reasonably efficient so the future should hold further possibilities especially when, as they all trooped off the field in high spirits at such a crushing defeat of old rivals – there came a gruff "Well dun boy", from Big Wally which lifted Jim's feet a further six inches off the ground.

On returning home his first job was to clean his muck-bespattered school boots with rainwater from the catchment barrel by the coal and wood barn – which also gave shelter from Father Bates's all-seeing eye, for he would be most displeased to discover that yet *another* son had started down the slippery slope of sport which could bring nothing but trouble in so many ways.

Jim slept but little that night, alone in his tiny, too short, bed, under the low sloping ceiling. The older ones shared a double bed and the floor – all within the one small bedroom; who would *want* to sleep, anyway, after such a momentous day? Far better to stay awake and try to relive the events over and over again – and to spare a thought for Tom Green whose absence had made it all possible in the first place. Also the noises in the thatch only inches above his head were not without interest; the sparrows frequently muttering and arguing as they jostled to find their favourite sleeping quarters; and the mice scampering up and down their well-worn tunnels within the dry, warm straw – which provided homes for so many creatures, some nice and some very nasty.

Once more that season Jim was called upon to forsake the scorebook and join his elders on the field of battle. Again, he made no noticeable impact on the match – although he *did* manage to carry a bat as far as the crease this time, hoping desperately, that the pad lashed to his left leg would hide the trembling in his knees; in the event, he didn't actually face a delivery – the dismissal of Bill at the other end brought the Shappley innings to a close, leaving Jim on 'Not Out Nought'. As he proudly accompanied his Captain back to the rest of the applauding team he hardly knew whether to be pleased or sorry that he still hadn't *really* been underfire.

His first season as official scorer, therefore, resulted in very little that could be called genuine achievements – but, to young Jim it had been choc-a-bloc with interest and excitement.

CHAPTER SIX

Harvest Time

It was unfortunate, of course, that harvest time clashed with cricket regularly every year but, as both events depended on warmer weather and longer days, this sad fact had to be accepted and put up with. The actual gathering and stacking of the corn, in general, began usually in late July and went on deep into August – in a wet season even into September. The word 'Harvest' meant much more, however, than corn; There was also a harvest, hopefully, from the large personal vegetable gardens to be dug, picked, or cut; crops which played a very important part in feeding the family: a supply of new potatoes with mint sauce, peas and beans straight from the pod, carrots and fresh crisp lettuce and etc. gave the summer months an added pleasure: whilst the various greens, and stored summer produce, kept the people reasonably fed during the harsh winter months, at very little cost – except, that is, in the many hours of extra labour demanded of the man of the house and his sons; Mr Bates, like many more, frequently caught up with his digging by operating at night by the light of the moon.

Young Jim's introduction to the harvest field came at the age of two or three, when he was dragged off by 'Mrs B' to 'Badgers-End' field carrying more food and drink to Mr Bates and George to keep them going until the light failed and they could work no longer. At this age he hated the whole business – the hideous noise of the Self-Binding Machine drawn by three sweating horses, going round and round the slowly decreasing area of standing corn – the frequent bangs of the farmer's double barrelled gun, as he potted the terror stricken rabbits driven from their cover, were most frightening.

As he grew older, however, all these things became interesting and exciting so that much of the school holiday was spent, with other children, in and around all the harvest work, (except, of course, for Saturday afternoons when an even greater pleasure demanded his attendance!). There were rabbits to be chased over and around the sheaves and shocks – but only on the sides clear of the farmer and his gun. There were also various other wild denizens of the corn-fields that were rudely driven from their homes and, as the uncut patch in the middle became smaller and smaller, so their terror grew and the safety of the surrounding hedges further and further away – 'To flee or not to flee?'

These halcyon days soon passed, however, and by the time he reached nine or ten years old he was gradually drafted into being useful instead of a nuisance. The first job was to pick up the sheaves left by the 'Binder' and set them up on end into 'Shocks' of half-a-dozen or so – in order that any rain during the following days (until carting could begin) could more readily run off.

His next step was 'Driving Heap' when the gathering actually began. This involved quite a big step in life's development for the boy because he now took charge of a horse for the first time. Although he'd been in and around farms and horses a good deal in the past – this was his first opportunity to take one of these gentle giants in hand by himself.

Luck was with him on the very first day of this new adventure – firstly, one of the two men assigned to his particular part of the field was brother George – never in a hurry, always cheerful and most unlikely to shout at, or find fault with, his young driver. George's job, incidentally, entailed throwing the sheaves up onto the cart, with his pitchfork, where his mate 'Ned' carefully built them into a firm, well balanced load, that would withstand the journey across the field and up the rutted lane to the stack, without shaking off.

The second slice of luck was of great importance insofar that Jim's mighty four-legged partner for most of the day was 'Kitty' – a shire mare of intelligence, kindness and beauty; physically she was a rich glossy dark brown – with three white socks and a handsome white blaze.

George explained to Jim what his duties were 'Jist 'old this 'ere chap-rein loose loike in yer 'and, Boy, *she'll* foller', and the little party set off across the stubble to the far end of the field. The rattling of the cartwheels over the rough sun-baked ground making a mockery of George's whistling. Jim could barely reach the bridle grip at Kitty's mouth, for the more tricky bits of guiding, except by standing on tip-toe so she obligingly lowered her head to make things easier for him as she plodded placidly on.

And so the day began in earnest, the first 'shock' being loaded – one sheaf at a time – then they all moved on 15 yards or so and stopped at the next one: Jim was not quite sure when, exactly, to start off each time because there was 'Ned up on high' to consider – he might easily be thrown off if the cart started before he was prepared – but Kitty knew well enough, she'd been through all this boring business every summer for many years and gave Jim a gentle nudge on the shoulder with her velvety pink nose and set off to the next stop.

At the fifth or sixth Shock there came a sudden flash of brown and white as George stuck his fork into the first sheaf and yelled "Goo orn Jim Boy, after 'im"' Jim plunged off immediately in pursuit of the startled rabbit but was never really in with any chance of success – partly because of his heavy hob-nailed boots and partly because the rabbit cleverly turned and twisted between the still standing shocks on its way to the safety of the hedgerow.

Gradually Kitty taught the new boy his job by lowering her head to nudge when it was time to move on and stopping at the required spot quite regardless of whether the tremulous command of "Whoa Kitty" came at the right moment or not. Obviously, therefore, she could do this starting and stopping routine perfectly well on her own and, in fact, often did – but she knew, just as the farmer knew, that this was all valuable experience for the boy in readiness for the future.

Dinner was taken on the shady side of a hawthorn hedge and after George helped Jim put Kitty's nose-bag on they all settled down for a peaceful rest – concentrating on their menus of oats and water for the horse – bread, cheese, raw onions and cold tea for the humans – ten all told.

Early in the afternoon another rabbit exploded from cover – *this* time Jim went off almost as quickly and achieved some success, but only because the victim made the mistake of heading into the open part of the field, which had already been cleared, and directly towards one of the other carting gangs whose shouts and waving arms brought confusion to the poor animal so that Jim was able to fall full length on it and make his first capture.

'Now what do I do?' he thought, 'I'm told to chase them but with no instructions as to what to do if I catch one!'

So, carrying the kicking and struggling rabbit by the ears he returned triumphantly to his cart – where George exclaimed...

21

"Well done me boy, yew've got a good dinner there f' termorrer noight".

With which he took it by the hind legs in his left hand and, with a chopping action with his right, broke the poor thing's neck.

"Shuv it in yer shirt f' now and give it to Mother when she brings the tea", he said, "An keep it owt of the Guv'ner's soight else '*e* moight wornt it".

After a few days 'driving heap' – mostly with Kitty – it dawned on Jim how she had looked after him by leading *him* whilst pretending to be led; he began bringing pieces of apple and carrots for her and they enjoyed regular 'conversations' about all sorts of things – unfortunately she seemed totally uninterested in cricket but, in general, she responded mainly with animated movements of those highly mobile ears which twisted and turned in all directions as he talked – as if in some kind of sign language of which, sadly, he was unfamiliar. The lad was disturbed by the cruel steel bit through her mouth but could think of nothing much to do about it – except to make sure never to pull on it in any way. He could, however, help considerably in keeping the horrible flies away from her eyes and nostrils – which would sometimes bring a nuzzle of gratitude in the back of his neck.

For three weeks that summer he did various jobs in the harvest fields, chased many rabbits – making very sure not to catch any! and continued always to long for Saturday to come round bringing the only thing better than the harvest fields and his new four-legged friend and mentor.

As the years passed his views on this changed because his summer holiday work schedules increased as he grew bigger and stronger. In fact, the very next year found him promoted to 'Driving Away', this entailed relieving the 'Driving Heap' boy of the fully loaded cart or waggon and leading the sweating horse out of the field, onto the narrow road, through more gateways and lanes, to the stack itself, being built by three more men. He then led an empty cart back to the field and so on all day. This wasn't too bad once he got the hang of negotiating the gateways whilst avoiding the horse's big front hooves when turning sharply. This latter problem was particularly difficult with 'Champ' between the shafts – unlike the placid shires he was a big rangy, grey ex-cavalry charger and was always in a hurry whether loaded or empty. With his splendid head held high and his big angry eyes – he became quite a frightening prospect for the eleven-year-old boy – especially when some unexpected noise or movement spooked him and caused his head to jerk up even higher with Jim hanging on in mid-air. How he avoided being trampled on as 'Champ' plunged through gateways and round corners was difficult to understand.

Finally, in his last year at school, the last of the Bates boys became an official full-time worker on a local farm for the full six weeks summer holiday from six in the morning to six at night and six to noon on Saturdays: at the end of which he received the sum of eight shillings – reduced to three after giving Mother Bates her share for housekeeping.

Nevertheless, he had no complaints because the farmer's wife fed him all kinds of goodies at any and every opportunity. As it turned out, however, he was not destined to make use of all that he'd learned in the fields – although he *did* make a point of seeing Kitty as often as possible – until the knacker's lorry eventually took her away to be put down through old age; an event which Jim took great care to miss and continued to wonder how many other small half-frightened boys that wonderful 'Lady of the Harvest Field' had prodded and nudged into confidence and companionship.

A Harvest Scene of the 20's and 30's. Note the cold tea can.

Father Bates ready for the day's work.

The furnace and Moulding Shed – where Jim spent the first part of his working life.

CHAPTER SEVEN

From Boy to Man

There were to be considerable changes in store for young Jim before the next cricket season spread its glow upon the land. In the Autumn he attained the all important age of fourteen years and had to make the big and sudden transition from boy to man – from leaving school on Friday to working in the small local iron foundry on Monday at 7.30 a.m.

One of the biggest factors in this week-end metamorphosis was both physical and psychological in its effect. This concerned the disappearance from public view of his bony, chapped knees. For practical reasons it was necessary to wear men's type overalls over his shorts for work and now, being a 'bona fida' wage earner, he could wear long trousers for evenings and weekends. These he had already acquired, by saving odd sixpences from the milk carrying contract, during recent months – plus the residue of the pay from working full-time on the farm throughout the six weeks of the school summer holiday; even after handing over five shillings to Mrs Bates the remainder went a long way towards the beautiful pair of grey flannels, with the knife-edge creases, that would be the envy of his mates and signify his becoming a man of substance.

The ever-present need for more income into the household budget precluded any hope of Grammar School or further education for Jim. Father Bates had completely vetoed the schoolmaster's advice, so, like many other boys and girls of the time, earning must come first. This in itself was no great shock or hardship for, as far back as he could remember, there had always been work waiting for him.

The next big change was, indeed, a joyous one; he became sole owner of his first 'bike'. It was probably third or fourth hand, battered, bent, and devoid of all the usual appendages devised for luxury travel – such as three speed gears, lights, saddle bag, pump, or carrier; the worn saddle was there, however, two wheels, rusty frame and handlebars, plus a creaky propulsion unit of pedal and chain.

Although nine shillings was not going to be easy to find from his weekly wage, the new owner was more than satisfied. Whole new horizons opened up for him immediately; important among them being the new found ability to participate in the activities of the 'Men's Club' on Saturday evenings during the long, dreary winter months – when the village hall became a veritable paradise of darts, table-tennis, cards, billiards and other delights; often described, hitherto, in great detail by his elder brothers who were, of course, all regular members.

The fact that brother Jack was instrumental in finding out about 'The Bike' being for sale may, or may not, have had any connection with him being rather fed up with carrying his fidgety young brother on his cross-bar to and from various places – including cricket matches.

Now the required age had been reached and rejoicing in the ownership of his own transport (give or take a few bits and pieces!) Jim was free to bike to Shappley on the dark winter evenings in company with his elders. First though, some kind of front light had to be acquired or devised for the machine in question and, here again, good fortune came to the rescue. It so happened that brother George had just decided to splash out seven-and-sixpence on "One of these 'ere new fangled carbide lamps, a big heavy imposing chromium plated affair in which a certain amount of dry carbide was put into one compartment and water in another, so that carefully controlled fusion between the two, produced a gas which, when ignited, resulted in a brilliant white light. A magnificent looking device, fairly reeking with opulence and acetylene fumes arrogantly displacing the poor, but more homely, 'Bacon Frier' – a simple paraffin and wick job in a cheap tin case, giving a light that barely outreached the front wheel and was highly prone to get blown out on windy nights but good enough for Jim's new steed, giving him the freedom of the king's of highway night or day.

This new age-status also justified his attendance at the Cricket Club's Annual General Meeting held in late November (more on this anon). Also, being a wage-earner gave automatic right, now, to read the one and only newspaper allowed into the Bates residence;

26

there were two reasons for this apparently unwarranted luxury of a Sunday newspaper – firstly, the paper afforded *its* readers a fire insurance free, in return for the weekly tuppence, and, secondly, it was a large sheeted edition of non-glossy texture and, therefore, ultimately, served a very important role in the little wooden hut at the end of the garden behind the blackberry bush. So, by Monday evening, when everybody else had finished with it, Jim avidly searched the back page for any cricket news – even though it was now wintertime – the M.C.C. party was touring the West Indies and sometimes the reports might include an action photograph of a batsman. After reading the scores in every detail he studied these pictures of the great men Hammond, Leyland, and others, long and hard, noting, particularly, the position of the head and the feet in relation to the ball and the stroke being played.

After some months of this study he began to realise that something was awry somewhere on the question of batting technique; the great players, as depicted in the paper, plainly used quite different methods than those of Shappley and other village batsmen. This apparent gulf seemed to go unnoticed and unmentioned by anyone else so he was reluctant, as a mere boy, to make any observations on the matter. In general the local batsmen tried to hit the ball without moving the feet from the original stance position on or outside the line of leg stump – therefore hitting the short ball airily towards Cover or Point, whilst the pitched-up delivery, hopefully, sailed over Long-On by a natural golf-like swing – whereas the experts seemed always to move their feet, and position – most frequently plumb in front of the stumps so as to play a variety of leg-side shots and, sometimes, appeared to be playing the ball from a position *outside* the off-stump' Of course, Jim accepted that their flat, true pitches and fast, close shaven outfields had much to do with this difference in approach, where a batsman could score boundaries, with ease, all along the turf, merely by deflections and cuts – and the ball didn't have a mind of its own off the wicket, causing one to shoot past the ankles and the next to whizz past the chin! Nevertheless, the fact that these first-class players could bat all day, sometimes, making a hundred runs individually and where half centuries were commonplace led young Jim to believe that there must be *some* advantage in trying to adopt their methods into the village cricket scene. He felt a trifle guilty at these traitorous thoughts, having been already striving to emulate his local heroes whenever an opportunity occurred.

CHAPTER EIGHT

Unwanted Extras – The Flies

Considering the various disincentives involved in village cricket in the 1930's it is somewhat surprising that it survived – and in many cases – prospered. Obviously the semi-feudal system familiar with the times had much to do with it providing, of course, the local Squire or 'Lord of the Manor' was sympathetic to the cause. Nevertheless, there were many difficulties left for the players themselves to contend with:- the laborious fence dragging business before and after every match; the cows and their everlasting mess and smells; the atrocious pitches hacked out of virgin meadowland with the accompanying long grass of the outfields, which made fielding such hard and dirty work. By general consent, however, the worst of the anti-cricket problems was the flies'. These pestilent creatures lived on live beef and, what might loosely be described as beef extract, for most of their evil lives and, consequently, were extremely tough and persistent – never more so, it seemed, than during a cricket match being played in, what *they* plainly considered to be, their own territory. "Who, and what, are these white clad figures daring to invade this private property belonging to us and our cattle? We will gather in our millions and drive them back whence they came", the evil things seemed to say.

Then these ill-natured creatures piled on the misery – each player, whether standing still or running, carried with him at all times an attendant dark angry cloud – settling first on any fresh steaming cow-pat then making straight for the nearest human ears, eyes and nostrils, so vulture-like in their persistence that a wave of the hand had no effect – they had to be physically knocked off the skin like winged leeches – only to zoom straight back in again to some other sensitive spot.

Whilst the ordinary fielders, with both hands free, were able to put up a reasonable resistance the poor Wicket keeper was in a sorry plight with his clumsy gloves making effective retaliation impossible. On some of the worst hot sultry days an observer from Town might well have been puzzled in seeing fifteen men out there continually flapping their ears and faces as if suffering some kind of eternal fit in this never-ending unequal battle against the Cattle Fly.

The two umpires enjoyed one small advantage over the players insofar that, with no running to do, they could poke sprigs of certain leaves possessing antifly properties, in or around their hats and so obtain a measure of relief.

The plight of the cows was pitiful to see – with their only weapon of defence being a tail which mother nature, in her so-called wisdom, had fixed at the wrong end. The Flies swarmed with impunity around the poor animal's eyes and nostrils; they were such easy prey, as they tried to graze and chew the cud amongst the lush grass and thistles, that from time to time the match may be held up for a while as the tortured beasts stampeded blindly across the field, with tails held high, in a desperate attempt to escape the tormentors. If, perchance, the charge should be in line with the pitch – then six fielders would quickly grab a stump each to fend off, or divert, the attack to more open spaces until, eventually, the panic died down and grazing began once more.

The horses seemed rather more intelligent by standing side by side in reverse order, under the chestnuts, so that each swishing tail guarded a neighbour's face. Despite this and other, problems the men and boys of the village were tremendously keen on their cricket – looking forward to it throughout the long winter months and facing the challenge with more laughs than moans.

CHAPTER NINE

The Cricket Club Annual General Meeting

Yet another new adventure for young Jim, and his new long trousers, came during the winter, when he attended the Cricket Club's A.G.M., an event he'd heard discussed, by his elder brothers, in previous years and was most anxious to see and hear for himself the mysterious rites that it seemed to embrace.

Naturally, like almost everything else, it took place in the Village Hall, on a cold November Saturday immediately prior to the normal Men's Club evening, thus ensuring a reasonably good attendance and saving an extra winter's bike ride for those who lived in the satellite hamlets. It should be noted here that the playing membership was about fourteen – the 'about' being explained by the one or two elderly gentlemen, whose playing days were officially over, but would sportingly turn out on the odd occasion when the team situation was desperate.

During the recent season the most usual Eleven consisted of:-

CAPTAIN BILL MILLER
> Taciturn but liked and respected by all. A 'stopper' behind the stumps rather than a wicket-keeper and could often hold an end up with the bat down at number seven or eight.

GEORGE BATES
JACK BATES
RALPH BATES
> These three – already described – obviously formed, collectively, an important element in the side.

BOB GREEN
TOM GREEN

Brothers who could never agree on *any*thing and liked to argue before, during, and after, every match but two very handy middle-order batsmen, for all that, unless they happened to be at the wicket together, a situation Bill Miller tried to avoid. Good fielders.

FRED OWEN

Opening bat, businesslike and with little to say, possibly due to his occupation as a gamekeeper with its attendant solitude.

Then comes

PHIL TODD

Jack of all trades, both on the cricket field and in his working life where he might be found sweeping chimneys on Monday and Tuesday, thatching a cottage or barn Wednesday, Thursday and Friday – with Saturday morning set aside for killing and drawing a neighbour's pig. All this capped with a deadly skill with the 'arrers' in the 'Dog and Duck' or the Men's Club.

The two main bowlers, who often bowled throughout the innings were:-

ALF MARSH

Right arm, whippy medium pace, accurate enough to claim most of his victims by hitting the stumps; also well capable of one or two 'sixes' at crucial moments.

WALLY STANTON

Also naggingly accurate medium pace – with hands so huge that he was known, far and wide, as 'Big Wally', or 'Shovel-Mitts' – an apt nickname, indeed, because those same bowling hands wielded a heavy shovel or pickaxe for most of the week. When he held the cricket ball clasped in one hand it disappeared from sight.

As no village cricket team can be really complete without the local Blacksmith – we come to:-

CHARLIE BOOTH
Although Charlie was stocky and – immensely strong – he did not conform to the fiction writer's traditional fierce fast bowler frightening his victims to vacate the crease with haste and relief at the first possible opportuny – no, instead, he buttressed the higher batting order with power and good sense, turning his arm over only on rare occasions.

And so, on the evening in question some eight or nine of these worthy yeomen were seated in a semi-circle facing 'The Table', at which sat the Squire himself as President. On his left, surrounded by a mess of papers and ledgers, was the elderly Schoolmaster, who, although no cricketer had been pressed, for many years, into the dual role of Secretary/Treasurer. After scrabbling amongst the assorted papers for some time for the evening's agenda – without any apparent success Mr Pickering deftly changed his spectacles yet again (bifocals having yet to be invented), and the meeting began.

Jim was both surprised and fascinated by this exhibition of nervousness by the same man who ruled the lives of sixty children so firmly during the school week. Perhaps it was due to his proximity to the 'Great Man' on his right who would shortly be firing questions at him and expecting quick factual answers.

The Squire, it must be said, did a great deal for the Club throughout the season in financial terms, paying for all the teas at home matches and supplying all kinds of material assistance, from his estate, in the form of posts, wire, manpower and so on, whilst his annual 'fiver' in the kitty made all the difference between solvency and disaster.

The Honorary Secretary then gave his Report, having illustrated again that the continual interchanging of spectacles frequently failed to synchronise with his immediate requirements. Nine Matches Won, Eight Lost, and Five Cancelled through rain, harvest, or other unspecified reasons. Next came the individual averages which caused so much lively discussion among the, assembly that the President was forced to call the meeting to order and allow the Schoolmaster to change hats, so to speak, and give his Treasurer's Report. This revealed a healthy enough Balance in hand of seven pounds, sixteen shillings and five pence – quite sufficient to elicit a unanimous show of hands in favour of adoption – much to the relief of the Honorary Secretary/Treasurer whose main paper searching should now be over for the evening.

The meeting was then thrown open for 'Any Other Business' and one of the elders, who had so far appeared to be asleep, sprang into verbal action to ask loudly "Since we got 'nuff money in the kitty, I reckon we should splash out on a new ball".

"Old ard", said Charlie, "We've only 'ad this 'un a coupla' seasons".

"Mebby so", returned the questioner, "But 'ass bin in the ditch twoice this year as *I* know on, an' that doon't dew a ball no good – gittin' all wet an' that".

Other voices immediately struck up to take sides in this important issue which this particular gentleman flung into the arena every year – probably for this very purpose rather than from any *real* interest in cricket balls, old or new, because once the argument became well established, Jim noticed that the instigator settled back in his chair and returned to sleep. Bob and Tom Green automatically took opposite sides – Bob claiming the ball to be a 'three-year-old' whilst Tom was sticking to two. There were those who disagreed, also, on how many times it *had* been in the ditch – 'Had the ditch been dried up or full of water at time of splashdown?' Some swore to four times in the last two seasons – could even remember and describe each occasion with self-satisfied detail – having been the ones who clouted it there – or so they claimed. Others recounted certain matches and named opposing batsmen who had caused the tell-tale splashes in the ditch and gained six runs in the process. All in all, therefore, this item alone could have occupied the meeting until midnight – and still the mischief maker slept on in contented oblivion.

The Squire, of course, had chaired many similar gatherings in the past, so after allowing some fifteen minutes or so of "I know it *was*" and "I know it *wornt* then", to flow back and forth, he rapped the table with sufficient force to bring about an abate-ment – not quite cessation – because each of the Green brothers were determined, as usual, to have the last word – but there continued "I know it *did*", and "I know it din't then" exchanges, were sufficiently subdued for the meeting to grind on.

The Honorary Secretary/Treasurer hurriedly changed glasses, more through nervous anticipation as to what may come next than definite need. "How much does a new ball cost Mr Pickering?" barked the Squire; this caught the Schoolmaster completely on the wrong foot as he had cleverly sneaked a look in the minutes book to find the *purchase date* of the current ball and had the answer "three years" prepared – *now* another search was called for to find the wretched *price*! 'Ho hum' he thought, 'Roll on Monday morning when there will only be sixty children to contend with'. Another quick scrabble and a quite brilliant fast optical swop operation revealed the new answer.

In the end, it was agreed that Three-and-Sixpence would be allocated for a new ball to start next season. George Bates, who reckoned he "Moight 'ev ter goo inter Town sometime threw the winter for a new boike tube", volunteered to attend to the actual purchase.

It was next agreed unanimously (much to the relief of Mr Pickering), that Annual Subscriptions remain at the current level of five shillings for adults and half-a-crown for those under twenty-one. Blacksmith Charlie Booth agreed to see what he could do about repairing the pads and, suffering various ribald comments such as "A few nuts an' bolts'll put 'em roight Charlie", or "A touch o' welding 'ere an' there p'raps". He also volunteered to take the mower under his muscular 'wing' for close season maintenance.

Before the meeting closed completely the Squire proposed, and led from the chair, a vote of thanks to Mr Pickering whose retirement from teaching came due at the end of the autumn term when he aimed to depart to a bungalow in Dorset. Consequently this was to be his last official connection with the Shappley Cricket Club.

The gathering then broke up, allowing the men to now enjoy the billiards, table-tennis and etc. for the remainder of the evening; Bob and Tom Green to continue their feud at the bridge table, the Squire to courageously accept a mug of cocoa with, and made by, the ex-Honorary Secretary/Treasurer, and Jim to simply wander around – supremely happy just to be there.

CHAPTER TEN

The Breakthrough

During that winter young Jim pondered long and hard on the question of how best to approach his all important future ambition to become a run-maker. Then fate took a hand in the person of Mr Arthur White – the newly appointed schoolmaster – replacing the retired Mr Pickering.

A tall angular man, Mr White was comparatively young and the father of several school-age children.

When springtime came round he let it be known that cricket was one of his many interests and had 'Played a bit at College'. His dialect labelled him, immediately, as a 'Furriner' and time revealed that he belonged to the deep south – Hampshire way. So with that inbuilt disadvantage and his delicate academic's hands, he, plainly, had much to overcome before being accepted into the tough hurly-burly of village cricket and, indeed, village life as well. His acceptance was greatly assisted, however, by two things – first, he readily agreed to take on the dual position, in the Club, of Secretary/Treasurer – vacated by the good Mr Pickering, and secondly, he owned a 'Stand-Up' Austin Seven car! which the committee secretly estimated would be most helpful for transporting the club kit and possibly, the overweight and slightly arthritic Joe, the umpire, to away matches. Joe had been finding the longer journeys of five or six miles by bike something of a struggle in recent years.

There being no boot to this particular Austin model – the bag it was hoped, would just about fit onto the back seat. In the event, both these possibilities worked out very well as the season progressed – to the benefit of the rest of the team who could now pedal more freely on machines no longer festooned with various pads and bats. Their greenish-white cricket boots still dangled from the handle-bars or round their necks but that was no great problem. Why greenish-white? Well, this had a direct connection with the cows and their natural habits, no amount of chalk and water would ever prevent that green showing through.

So far very little had been said about the new man's actual cricket ability but the old adage about 'Not looking a gift horse in the mouth' was readily invoked by the selection committee which, bearing in mind the man's ability to walk and breathe regularly had no hesitation in putting him in for the first match.

Our hero, meanwhile, felt even more excited this year as the days slowly wound round to cricket time once again. Although still the official scorer he was beginning to look a bit more like a man, rather than a boy in long trousers, and thus freely accepted. Socialising with most of the team members at the Men's Club through the winter months, plus having his own transport, must go a long way, he thought, towards his longed for and eventual inclusion into the team itself in the next year or two. For the time being he paid his half-crown membership fee – sharpened his new full length pencil, kept the scorebook to the best of his ability and helped with all the odd jobs he could lay his hands on.

In his first innings for the Shappley team, batting at Number Six, the Schoolmaster made only five singles but his manner of making them was decidedly odd – causing much 'Tutting' and many critical remarks from his new team mates; Jim, however, could scarcely believe his eyes – here he saw many resemblances to his precious newspaper photographs – almost as if they were coming to life out there only seventy yards away. To begin with, Mr White was quite fussy when preparing for his innings – two pads firmly fixed, his own batting gloves appeared from a small bag and, in light of subsequent events, it was suspected by some that the same bag had concealed a 'Box', only *suspected*, because he was never seen to put one on or take one off.

Watched with extreme interest, therefore, by all the Shappley team, and the three pundits adorning the fallen tree by the boundary, Mr White straight away put Joe in a tizzy by requesting 'Middle-and-leg' guard' "Everybody knows that 'Middle' is the roight an' proper guard" Joe murmured to himself, aloud he said "Eh, whadjer say sir?" just to give the batsman an opportunity to rectify his mistake; 'middle-and-leg please" came the repeated request and, as Joe was now shuffling his feet and in some difficulty – the Schoolmaster turned and pointed with a gloved finger to the stumps in question, to which the worthy and well-meaning umpire responded "Oh ah, Oh ah, yew war'nt them tew dew yer? roight y'ar then", and proceeded cautiously and, with complicated instructions, to that end. Whether or not the Hampshire man really received that for which he had asked was probably doubtful, but certainly Joe had an odd tale to recount to cricketing friends for a week or two.

Play recommenced and the new recruit's peculiar ways soon became evident. To begin with he moved quite deliberately into the path of the ball – this courageous but foolhardy act was accompanied by a forward lunge with the left leg and bat – as a result of which he lay writhing on the ground clutching his ribcage with both hands whilst asking, quite calmly, if his spectacles were safe. Once again play restarted but, it appeared, no lesson had been learned – he persisted in his ways and, next over, was felled again by a blow to the midriff – followed later by a sickening thud in the 'unmentionables' which strangely, it seemed to the fielders gathered round, caused only minor discomfort and gave off an odd sound quite unlike human flesh. Nevertheless it was noticeable to the discerning eye (Jim's of course!) that the man placed his bat squarely to the ball far more often than anyone else ever did, so that with the help of his body and sheer courage, appeared able to defend his wicket all day – barring shooters. He made little or no attempt to really swing at the ball or hit in the air so his five singles came from pushes and glances which, although stopped immediately by the surrounding long grass, were occasionally sufficient to allow the batsmen to change ends.

This remarkable innings became the main talking point of the day – there came much shaking of heads amongst the critics and doubts were voiced as to how long the poor man would remain out of 'Orspittal and who would run the school and play the church organ when the seemingly inevitable serious accident occurred.

Jim's dilemma, to a large extent, still remained, insofar that whilst he had actually *watched* a batsman practising the methods used by the masters in the newspaper photographs, the penalties seemed rather harsh on pitches such as these. Should he still follow the traditional village ways and be satisfied with becoming a good Shappley batsman scoring maybe 150 runs a season and being much the same as the others?, or should he take the plunge and follow the example of Mr White? On the one hand he couldn't help feeling there must be a reason why this particular teacher had landed up in this particular time in Jim's cricket career; on the other hand he didn't much fancy all the physical pain and bruises that would obviously ensue – especially during the months and, possibly, years of learning. "Of course", his inner voice insisted, "The painful aspect will only last whilst you're playing on rough village pitches; once you become a regular member of the Middlesex team and play at Lords you'll be alright". Ah, the dreams of youth.

In the end he resolved to wait and see; it seemed probable that he would not be going to the 'middle' much, if at all, for this season and could afford the time, therefore, to sit back and watch the new man for the remaining months then, perhaps, arrive at a decision by September. He must certainly ignore the more general opinion amongst the members that "The 'Ampshire man is a bluddy cricketing nutter".

As things turned out, the youngest of the Bates boys was called upon no less than four times, that summer, to make up the eleven; mostly due to last minute emergencies – but *once*, during the usual harvest-time problems, his name appeared on the official Team Sheet pinned up on the Village Hall notice board – so on *that* occasion he was able to savour his luck and dream his dreams for four whole days and four nights.

The first actual run ever to come from his bat and be recorded for posterity, was an accidental edge which somehow became sufficiently entangled in the long grass that a single was just possible before second slip could oblige. The very next ball he received from the other end clipped the bails high over the 'Keeper's' head and they all walked off: what matter! it's in the book in black and white – 'J. Bates, Bowled Wallace, 1'. Of course he tried hard to conceal his jubilation and pride, especially as no fewer than four of his elders and betters failed to trouble the scorers at all!

During the laborious business of dragging the fence back for re-erection around the square, he dashed around with tremendous enthusiasm – with feet only occasionally touching the ground – visualising already the great things that might happen when the next call came, now that this giant step forward had at last been made. Alas and alack, after several weeks of fidgeting impotently at the scoring table, his next opportunity to shine ended in disaster – clean Bowled for Nought.

A fresh, up and coming, young lad took over the pitch protection job so Jim now regularly accompanied the men, on their meandering stroll to the Village Hall, for a proper sit-down tea. He sat at the end of the long trestle table with a plate and knife all to himself and was offered the various plates of goodies whenever he appeared ready for more. The presence of the knife puzzled him at first until, suddenly, he espied the jar of home-made blackberry jam half hidden by the Captain's elbow at the other end of the table and, by continually staring at it, with knife in hand, someone finally caught on and the luscious looking jar found its way down the table. There were also cups of tea brought round by the good ladies so, all in all, this was luxury indeed.

CHAPTER ELEVEN

The Poor Fielders

Of the many differences between cricket played in rural areas and that played on properly prepared grounds in towns, big schools, colleges, and the like – fielding was, by far, the biggest.

The batsman had his problems by having to compete against the pitch and the outfield, as well as the bowler, in his search for runs; whilst the latter, consequently, gained considerably, he need not worry much about swing, turn, flight, or even pace – he had only to bowl reasonably straight avoid the full-toss and leave the rest to the bumps, plantains, and dandelions.

The outfield at Shappley conformed to the usual standard – a patchwork of quite closely cropped pathways meandering in and around large areas of long, tangled grass sprinkled with nettles, docks, and thistles, anything from one to three feet high. The unfortunate fielder, therefore, found himself forever faced with a choice of two evils, so to speak, if the ball landed in a tangled clump there would be difficulty in finding it, whilst if it ended up in view, on the shorter cropped part, then there were the "cowflops" to contend with – that inevitable trail left behind as the animals chewed their way back and forth every day. If he struck particularly unlucky his darting eyes may well spot the ball nestling happily in the middle of a fresh sloppy deposit. Jim remembered his first encounter with this messy situation – on the day he'd been long-stop – the ball flew high over the slips, from a top edge, and landed somewhere in the third man area; as always, once landed – disappearing from sight. Jim raced towards the spot, endeavouring to keep in mind the exact clump of thistles, and, at the same time, watch where his feet were going. On arrival there was no ball to be seen, then, suddenly he spotted the tell-tale lump in the middle of a fly-covered pile; with shouts of "Cummorn boy,

The Village Hall where cricket teas were enjoyed and a variety of village functions held.

The Church and War Memorial.

CRICKET in the long

ting by the author).

SHAPLEY CRICKET CLUB V — C.C. CLUB

HOME CLUB .... VISITORS Shapley

1st INNINGS OF Shapley PLAYED AT .... ON July 14th 1936

		RUNS SCORED	HOW OUT	BOWLER	TOTAL
1	F Owen		L.B.W.	E Newman	2
2	J Bates		Bowled	E Newman	3
3	F Todd		Run Out		1
4	T Green		c Newman	Gravestock	0
5	C Beech		L.B.W.	Gravestock	1
6	A Marsh		Bowled	E Newman	1
7	B Blanton		Not Out		91
8	G Bates		c/bowled	Gravestock	0
9	R Bates		c Dayton	Newman	12
10	W Wilkins		Bowled	Newman	3
11	L Blanton		Bowled	Newman	5

BYES 1+1				
LEG BYES 1				
WIDE BALLS				
NO BALLS				

	TOTAL BYES	3
	TOTAL LEG BYES	1
	TOTAL WIDE BALLS	
	TOTAL NO BALLS	

TOTAL 122

RUNS AT THE FALL OF EACH WICKET	1	2	3	4	5	6	7	8	9	10
	4	5	5	4	8	11	12	94	93	122
OUTGOING BATSMAN										

The score card of "A Match to Remember"

44

less ' ev it then!" from all sides, the decision of boot or bare hands could not be delayed – but, even as he balanced on one leg to, somehow, roll the ball out of its warm home – Bob Green came charging in – grabbed it by hand, muck and all, and hurled it in to poor Bill Miller who instinctively accepted the throw in his gloves and consequently was bespattered over the face and shirt with blobs of green.

If the point of disappearance happened to be definitely in the long grass – those two or three men within seeing distance converged on the spot to probe and stamp around until someone either saw it or trod on it. In such instances it became necessary for one fielder of the group to keep a close watch on the batsmen so as to count how many times they crossed, the unwritten law being that if the batsmen were on their sixth run and the ball still not found the 'sentinel' fielder must shout 'Lost Ball' – otherwise they could go on running until the ball *was* found or until they got too tired to run anymore. The 'Lost Ball' call, however, made the match temporarily dead – the lucky striker credited with six runs and everybody, from both sides joined in the search, so that play might be restarted as soon as possible.

This rather strange but necessary rule, under the circumstances, is rather dramatically illustrated from a match played at Shappley. Set to score 33, after tea, The Home side began very badly – losing 3 Wickets For 2 Runs, then came a recovery by Bob Green and Charlie Booth who, with great care and good sense, inched the total into double figures and respectability – only for both to fall in consecutive overs, as is so often the case after a valuable stand. Phil Todd and Captain Bill strove to continue the good work but perished gallantly and, more importantly, uncomplainingly to blatantly dubious umpiring decisions. Alf Marsh struck one or two telling blows before being well and fairly caught at long on – so when Big Wally went in at number 10 with the score at 22 for 8 – all seemed lost. Perhaps a trace of complacency crept unconsciously into the visiting team. Then the initiative of Joe, the home umpire, in signalling a Wide and a No-Ball in one over helped things along. Soon one of Wally's wild swings made a half contact skying the ball towards Cover, some 30 yards from the pitch, the batsmen trotted through for an obvious single whilst fielders converged onto a particularly thick patch of long grass and thistles where the ball had been seen to land. As they searched amongst the tangled mass the Shappley pair sneaked another run, and another, and another; when eventually they turned for the sixth run the rest of the Home Team, up by the hollybush, restrained their excitement and remained very quiet – no shouts of "Cummorn Wally", or "Run 'em up". The fielders still stamped and poked away in their search – not yet really concerned, but it was this very nonchalance that brought about their team's downfall because they forgot to nominate a 'sentinel' to make the all important call of 'Lost Ball' at the appropriate moment. All of a sudden, a great cheer went up from the Shappley men – the searching fielders heads lifted as one – to see the umpires pulling up the stumps and walking off with the batsmen who had quietly negotiated Nine Runs off that one thick edge shot to Short Extra Cover and Shappley had won by One Wicket.

Fortunately, the opponents that day were a friendly lot and, after a spate of argument amongst themselves as to whose fault it was that nobody took on the job of 'Look-Out', they soon saw the humorous side of the episode and accepted defeat with fairly good grace.

There was *one* way, it must be said, whereby the cunning fielder may turn this particular environmental disadvantage to become his ally. Let us imagine the typical Summer Saturday afternoon over at Menin Cricket field with the cows and flies in their usual close attendance. The Home side is batting and the ball is lofted over to Midwicket where it disappears into a rough tangled patch; Bob Green first on the scene, plunges in amongst the thistles and, strangely, spots the ball straightaway – snuggled deep down amongst the grass roots, a quick glance up tells him that the batsmen are about to complete their second run so he gives no sign of his luck but continues stomping around, with head lowered, as if still searching. Under his eyebrows, however, he is watching every move of the two batsmen who are, of course, watching him with equal care. Suddenly they decide to chance a third run on the assumption that the ball is still lost – *that* is the moment at which Bob swoops on it and delivers it cleanly and swiftly to Bill who easily completes the run-out.

This ploy of gamesmanship by a fielder had to be very cleverly and delicately performed if the desired run-out were to be achieved – especially when two or three team mates dashed up to assist in the search for the ball, which to everyone else on the field, except Bob, was lost in the usual way because he now had to prevent them seeing the ball and giving the game away as well as carrying out his complicated bluff with the batsmen.

CHAPTER TWELVE

High and Low

From his vantage point as scorer Jim continued to watch, closely, the batting technique of the new comer. The poor chap still gathered his weekly crop of bruises but he also collected runs with remarkable consistency – 10 here, 8 there, and so on – which, in team totals of 30 or 40, were of considerable value; plus the fact that, more often than not, he occupied the crease longer than anyone else even allowing for time spent lying on the pitch rubbing various parts of his anatomy.

For some years, now young Jim had, quite naturally, expected to copy and follow his local heroes – ever since he'd been hanging around cricket matches and being involved, so coming to a decision to, change horses in mid-stream, became a very difficult one and a case of 'make-or-break'. If it went wrong he would look silly as well as suffer probable injuries for nothing, on the other hand a particularly fine photograph he'd seen recently, of Douglas Jardine playing a back defensive shot with his long nose exactly over the bat handle, finally tipped the scales and when, during late August, he was called upon at the last minute to replace a late drop-out for an away match at Westford, he determined to 'Give it a Go'. Finding two pads available helped to both make the decision and to quell some of his fears. Westford had made a useful 48 on a pitch less spiteful than most, due in part to the home club's custom of allowing a small flock of sheep the freedom to do a large part of the Groundsman work for him.

Shappley did not bat well and when the small number 11, carrying a bat much too big and heavy for him, joined Captain Bill at the crease 12 more runs were needed to win. Fortunately, at that period, the friendlier medium pace bowlers were operating and the mental effort of deliberately thrusting his left leg, body, and bat into the path of the speeding missile was, perhaps, slightly less than it might have been. Jim successfully negotiated the three remaining deliveries of the over with reasonable efficiency and immediately felt a foot taller – especially when he heard his eminent partner at the other end say "Well done boy, keep yer end up". Half-an-hour later they walked off together - both unbeaten to be greeted and accompanied by much applause from both teams - the required 12 runs having been scored in this unlikely but unbroken last wicket partnership. Above all, to one person in particular, the scorebook recorded, for all to see, 'Jim Bates, Not Out 4'. Among the various complimentary remarks thrown his way by other players, the one giving him the warmest glow came from Mr White with "The boy kept his bat straight anyway". A comment that our 'hero' filed away somewhere in his burgeoning mental cricket dossier.

His euphoria at this tremendous success lasted for several weeks; longer, thankfully, than it took for the various bruises to fade away. The one on the left hip-bone and another on the inside of the right thigh were the most difficult to disguise from Father Bates who, had he discovered them, may well have added a few more in a different place through the medium of a wide leather belt adorned with a heavy brass buckle.

Three weeks later Jim struck lucky again – this time as the players waited at the usual spot before setting off to do battle at Remston – the missing face was that of Fred Owen, the Game-keeper opening batsman – normally the most punctual of men. Bill, as usual, marched back and forth muttering and kicking stones and bikes alike more in frustration than anger – because, beneath that dour and sometimes complaining exterior – there smouldered a great love of the game. Eventually, with a last glance at the church clock. he said "Roight y'ar then, less goo, carn't wait no longer, the boy'll efter play".

So with the Schoolmaster leading the way in his four-wheeled tin box – bearing the ample form of Joe in the front and the club bag in the back the motley cavalcade took the road. There's not much to report on this match, spoiled to some extent by rain; the 'Boy' batting at number 11 was adjudged L.B.W. for nought after surviving for only 3 balls and so was brought down to earth with a bump as well as learning, the hard way, that this new way of batting also included the further disadvantage of making an L.B.W. dismissal much more likely. He also suffered some tongue lashing on arriving home with wet feet and the elegant grey flannels sodden up to the knees from fielding in the long wet grass.

He was now faced, therefore, with yet another dilemma – a sartorial one this time – unless something ingenious could be devised, the 'greys' would be quite unwearable next day for the usual 'Sunday Parade'. The other lads would snigger, and the girls probably giggle, at his discomfiture in showing nice sharp creases down to the knees then a mass of crumpled cloth dragging around the shoes. The alternative of reverting to shorts, of which he had a reasonable pair available, was even more unthinkable because of the humiliation involved. In the end he made some excuse to borrow the only candlestick, from his parents' bedroom that night, so that he could see to fold the trousers very carefully in the right creases and place them secretly under his mattress and, 'Hey Presto" next morning they were sufficiently dried and pressed to allow him to get by.

Also, on Sunday morning outside the Church, it was revealed by Mrs Owen, that the reason for her husband's failure to turn up for the match with his usual reliability, was that he suffered a most embarrassing accident on his way home from the woods (where the young pheasants were being reared) for a quick bite and change. Whilst negotiating a barbed wire fence, with a brace of rabbits in one hand and the double-barrelled twelve bore across his back, one boot slipped off the lower strand just as he was astride the top one.

" 'E tore 'is trowsis underneath", Mrs Owen disclosed then went on to explain to the group of listening cricketers, with her face growing redder by the minute, " 'E tore other things as well", she blurted out, "so 'e 'ad a job ter walk 'ome, let alone play cricket!" The explanation seemed to elicit little sympathy from the gathering – only ribald remarks and sly chuckles and poor Mrs 'O' quickly escaped when she spotted a friend wearing an interesting new hat sailing in through the Lytch gate towards them.

CHAPTER THIRTEEN

Still Undecided

Two more opportunities that season brought Jim a Single and yet another Nought Not Out – making a grand total of FIVE runs in FIVE innings – most disappointing, especially after that great day of glory at Westford, the memory of which was fast becoming dimmed. His resolution on the new batting approach also suffered a battering and doubts were again creeping in but, once again, fate managed to give him a little nudge towards the Schoolmaster's lead – possibly just in time.

It so happened that, right at the end of the summer, with a late harvest still in full swing, and players in short supply – even for a home game, Jim was first in line to fill a vacancy – only to learn that an urgent phone call by the Squire himself, resulted in procuring the services of one of his sons now on vacation from Oxford University. The dream that Jim had so often visualised – of walking out to the middle on the Home Ground was cruelly snatched from him at the very last minute after he had actually been *asked* to make up the depleted side only half-an-hour before starting time. He was hard put to keep his eyes from watering as he filled in the scorebook details – silently cursing such diabolical inventions as telephones and the fast car which, no doubt, would transport the young Squire from wherever he was back to Shappley in time to ruin Jim's day.

There were still lingering hopes, of course that the 'Bugatti' might break down or run into a ditch perhaps, but no, at the appointed time the deep-throated roar of his well-known car was heard and over the fence climbed the driver, having thrown his personal expensive cricket bag over first already changed, he looked quite magnificent, from white buckskin boots, cream flannels, cream shirt, blue and white striped blazer and a white silk scarf casually slung around his neck. The resentful scorer studied the beautiful ensemble and, rather maliciously, thought of the many lovely sloshy fresh cow-pats dotted about the field and hoped! He also hoped that the elegant interloper would prove to be quite useless as a cricketer and make such an ass of himself that he would never dare interfere again – Squire or no Squire; 'Oh dear', the bitterness of frustrated youth.

When the time came for the new number four to pad up, his long leather bag revealed a veritable Aladdin's Cave of cricket gear; watching the game with one eye and these preparations with the other Jim saw the beautiful pair of pads taken out, the gaudy peaked cap, batting gloves, his own personal bat and a cup-like contraption with leather straps attached which he might just be seen, behind the holly-bush, fixing between his legs and around the waist; 'So' Jim thought, 'Now we know what a 'box' looks like'.

Soon the moment came for the guest batsman to take his place at the crease and gradually the crestfallen scorer was forced to sit up and take very careful notice – to forget his disappointment and resentment because here again was his photographs coming to life before his very eyes! True the man was left-handed but all the same actions were there, in reverse; the same forward and across movements, the same back-lift and so on. After recording the first half-dozen runs very reluctantly Jim was forced, eventually, to enjoy watching this University chap carve his way to a most elegant and attractive 32 runs; so much so, that he joined whole-heartedly in the applause that greeted the returning hero not only for the intrinsic value of the innings – which had won the match but also – and, perhaps more importantly, his doubts had been swept aside once more. He must, *must*, make every effort, himself, to emulate these examples which, from time to time, were being displayed before him – as if for a specific purpose.

Jim now felt sufficiently strongly about it that he took the risk of taking Ralph into his confidence on the matter and, perhaps, seek his opinion if not advice. Ralph himself was doing pretty well as a middle order batsman and often seemed to give the art of batting rather more thought than the others – in fact, he fell somewhere between the two methods. It so happened, however, that Ralph's run-making ambitions were to become somewhat side-tracked before the next season arrived so again Jim postponed his actions indefinitely to see what transpired during the close season and the A.G.M.

51

CHAPTER FOURTEEN

New Captain New Era

As had been rumoured, the Annual General Meeting that autumn heralded the resignation of that worthy Captain, of many years, Bill Miller – which involved finding both a new Captain and a new wicket-keeper. It was the latter vacancy that drew Ralph's attention like, a moth to a candle. He had already – during the previous season – made it fairly obvious that he coveted those big battered gloves and, in fact, had actually done the job once or twice when Bill was absent for some reason. So with this exciting possibility in mind he probably decided, there and then, to let his batting take its natural course, for the time being and concentrate on trying to take over the seemingly thankless task of keeping wicket under circumstances in which the ball tended to fly off the pitch in any direction other than normal.

Bill's somewhat premature retirement from the game he so loved was, sadly, due largely to his horrible suffering during the Great War in which he spent three years in the mud, blood, and noise of trench warfare, so that at 51 he became physically and mentally an old man.

The post of Captain was filled with very little ado – thanks to heavy hints from the presiding Squire. Mr White, the Schoolmaster, with his completely different approach to the game, was elected without opposition, giving him yet another 'hat' to wear with his Honorary Secretary/Treasurer ones.

With the various other voluntary duties he undertook in the Parish – such as playing the church organ at all Sunday services and any other religious gatherings – many people wondered how he ever found time to do any teaching! However, the new Captain was happily accepted by one and all because the hardened, weather beaten village men, grudgingly, and secretly, had come to admire the way this relatively delicate and mild-mannered man worked his way into the rough and tumble of their football and cricket.

Once again, during 'Any Other Business', the same elderly member awoke from his usual doze to fire off the annual shot across the bows of the committee "What about a new ball then" Mr White, the new Schoolmaster Secretary/Treasurer, whose glasses, to everyone's relief, appeared to be more adaptable and remained 'in situ' under all clerical circumstances was quite unaware of the ritualistic aspect of the question and accepted it as being born of genuine concern. He was much surprised, therefore, at the immediate antagonistic reaction of the other members, such as – "Oh, shut up John!? or "Yew know we 'ad a new 'un larst year, yew old stirrer!" The Squire, nevertheless, asked for the minute book to be checked just to make sure, and there it was – in Mr Pickering's immaculate hand – "One New Ball 3s. 6d.". Consequently the proposal embodied in the question was turned down flat but, unfortunately, the arguments had once again been sparked off, in particular a new one, of a rather obtuse technical nature, between those regular protagonists – brothers Bob and Tom Green. Bob maintained that the frequent dunking into sloppy, still warm, cowpats caused much more harm to the ball than did the odd soaking through playing on a wet day or by a six-hit into the ditch: Tom naturally took the opposite view – insisting that the regular applications of said bovine waste matter was, in fact, most beneficial and helped to preserve the stitching. How long this novel and exciting new argument might have continued remains unknown because the inherent authority in the voice of the Squire brought it swiftly under control – if not to a complete close, the difference of opinion continued for a time but only at a muttering level. So, as the original questioner slipped back into oblivion, the meeting moved on to a similar, but less contentious matter calling for the need of a new scorebook; this item slipped through easily enough whilst the 'Greens' were still enjoying (sotto voce) their "I know it *does* then, "I know it doon't stage."

53

CHAPTER FIFTEEN

The Men in White Coats

Soon after becoming the team's scorer Jim began to realise how very important was the role played by the Umpire, in the average village cricket match. Much more important than their counterparts in the first-class game; although, like them, they were usually ex-players suffering from a bit of arthritis or back trouble perhaps, which had caught up with them in later years.

To understand properly the extraordinary different problems he was faced with – compared to the Umpire in a test-match, it is necessary to visualise the isolation and consequent interwoven fabric of their lives. When virtually the only means of travel was on foot or by 'push-bike'; therefore, footballers and cricketers could play only for the Village or Parish in which they lived – where they went to school, grew up, married, and eventually expired. Our typical village umpire then, would probably be related to at least half the team either by blood or marriage and one or two more working colleagues during the week and might even be adding his voice to others in the Church choir on Sundays.

Because of all this it was most difficult for the poor chap to give a Home batsman out 'L.B.W.' when, only the previous day, the same man had given up his whole evening to help put up the umpire's new chicken shed! or, indeed, another possible victim of the upraised finger who came round during the week with two score of fine, upstanding brussel plants, for which he refuses to accept any remuneration.

Consequently, decisions were often dictated by *who* was involved and which team would benefit rather than by the boring technical laws printed in the back of the scorebook.

54

Rivalry was another factor in the arbitrator's decision making:- if Umpire 'A' bagged six victims in the afternoon – three L.B.W., two Caught Behind, and one Run-out, perhaps, on behalf of his fielding team – then his opposite number would be looking for at least six and, hopefully, seven when *his* team were bowling.

It may be argued that, in theory anyway, one biased official cancelled out the other but, as every cricketer knows, this does not work out in practice.

There were, of course, *some* Umpires who were strong willed enough to be honest and unbiased even though they might suffer for it socially and domestically afterwards. A batsman given out 'L.B.W.' by his own Umpire felt extremely hard done by and doubly damned.

One or two amiable and well liked adjudicators could be found on the circuit, chaps who could get away with anything, for or against, by sheer humour or wit: 'Old Harry' who 'Stood' for Cottam, had developed the art even further by shouting a loud "Owzat?" himself when the ball hit the pad; his subsequent decision, however, still depended mostly on which side were batting.

Young Jim knew nothing of all this as yet, partly because he was not allowed into the local with the men after the match where the post-mortem arguments flourished. There would always be ample examples of dodgy decisions to be fought over and blame to be apportioned whilst, who scored the runs and who took the wickets was of secondary interest.

So, it will be seen, that in many cases the 'Man in White' was considered more as a member of the team than as a trusted neutral. This conclusion is underlined by the fact that when the Captain found himself short of a player, prior to an away match, and no means or hopes of getting a replacement – he preferred to take the field with ten players with the Umpire retaining his official position – rather than to invite the gentleman, (who was likely to be a handy player still), to become the eleventh man, thus leaving the umpiring open to all kinds of possible abuse. The thought of having *two* inhabitants of the Home village in charge of the match would have been quite untenable.

As one would expect, the one area of the game in which most village cricketers excelled, was their throwing: even Jack Hobbs, England's finest Cover Point of the day would have envied the skills and power of these men who had been throwing stones at hares, rats, birds and anything else that ran, crawled, or flew around the countryside, since their schooldays. Many a rabbit ended up in the oven through foolishly running head-long into a fast moving stone – and many a pigeon and pheasant saw nothing of the cause of his sudden downfall from the apparent safety of his lofty roost in the dusk of a quiet evening.

Therefore, run-outs, and near run-outs were a regular problem for the Umpires. One such instance to illustrate the point involved 'Old Joe', the Shappley official himself, whose ambling journey to a Home match took him, by a slightly devious route, into the backdoor of the 'Dog And Duck' and, some fifteen minutes later, out the front door and eventually, to the cricket field.

On the day in question, it was very plain that the outcome of the match depended, to a large extent, on the early dismissal of the opposition's number 3 – a most feared batsman called 'Jake' – blessed with an exceptionally keen eye, backed up with huge shoulders and arms to match. Already he had bludgeoned twenty or more forceful runs and all seemed lost for the Home side when suddenly he misjudged a second run. Tom Green, fielding somewhere around the long-on area, swooped on the ball which, for once, had landed in one of the shorter cropped patches, and smashed the wicket down with a direct fifty-yard throw with the pugnacious 'Jake' yards short of his ground. The Shappley team rose as one man in a loud and triumphant appeal to the square-leg umpire, the peacefully grazing cows lifted their tails high in the air and stampeded blindly at the sudden, ecstatic roar from eleven throats on the field plus three more watching elderly enthusiasts who sat, as usual, on a dead fallen tree, as near as dammit square with wicket in question. The rooks in the elms at long leg also took vociferous umbrage at this uncalled for interruption to their normal Saturday afternoon domestic affairs.

On the field of play a stunned silence followed that single outburst – simply because there was no Square-Leg Umpire in sight to offer a response! Even as the players looked at each other in silent bewilderment Joe's ample figure came into view, carefully negotiating the stile that led back from the spinney to the field, still attempting to do up his buttons and no doubt wondering what all the 'Hoo-Hah' was about. He was quickly and loudly informed of the situation by a number angry voices – chief amongst them, naturally enough, being that of Tom – whose mighty throw was responsible. Poor Joe knew not what to do for the best and could only repeat and over again – "I 'ad ter goo an 'ev a dror orf, I was bustin" The batsmen, meanwhile, were conferring with the Benton Umpire at the bowler's end and naturally insisted unanimously that "If the Judge is absent there can be no sentence", claiming with confidence and vigour that the charge of 'Run-out' must be dismissed rather than the blatantly guilty batsman.

Eventually the match recommenced under a very heavy psychological cloud and minus the services of Tom Green who stamped angrily off – snatched his jacket and brown shoes from the holly bush, where they always hung during play, and set off for home, pausing only to turn and shout "Doon't pick me when we play this lot ag'in – if ever we *dew*".

Benton won the match easily enough and the Schoolmaster Captain of the home side tried hard to patch things up but, not being a natural 'drinking man' he was handicapped from the start, for many harsh and earthy Barfordshire words had been said by various members of his team. So the Benton team mounted their bikes and set off home – well pleased with the victory, which more than compensated for minor things like being sworn at or being accused of cheating because their hero had not 'Walked'.

Joe had quietly slipped away, after one more brief visit over the stile, to the spinney.

CHAPTER SIXTEEN

The Decision is Made

So Jim continued to watch out for, and save, any newspaper photographs of famous batsmen in action, (keeping them well out of sight of Mr Bates), especially those coming back from Australia where the mighty Hammond, Bradman, Ames and others were piling up runs galore. 'What kind of supermen are they?' he thought, 'How *could* they bat all day – sometimes scoring a hundred, two hundred, or even *three* on occasion – off their own bats? Were their blades really only 4¼ inches wide as Shappley's were?' Even accepting, in the imagination, the vastly different and advantageous circumstances they enjoyed, there was still the much faster and better bowling, brilliant fielding and wicket keeping to contend with, which must go some way towards redressing the balance between the two games – similar in theory but so different in practice. The huge gap between them was too much for the lad, as yet, to fully understand. It was possible, he supposed, that these 'Gods' of the cricket field were born with extra physical attributes – such as abnormal eye-sight, reflexes, or co-ordination – but not really *likely*, better and more highly developed perhaps through constant practice, but not physically different, like having three eyes or two thumbs on each hand.

Continued pondering and puzzling led him to resolve, more strongly than ever, that his only hope of finding an answer was to stick to his aim of trying to copy their methods – even though the interim period was proving very sticky indeed.

Jim's laudable desire to play in a technically correct manner was shaken by an innings which became a legend in his time. It was a hot sultry day in mid July when the vicious cow-flies were accompanied by millions of thunder-flies, quite harmless and gentle of nature but so numerous as to add considerably to everyone's discomfiture and make life one continual scratch. In the middle of all this a quite remarkable cricketing event took place during a Shappley home match against Little Wells – old rivals and strong adversaries.

Harvest was in full swing and both teams suffered accordingly; indeed, had there been any means of communication between the two places available, the match may well have been cancelled. As it was, both sides managed to scrape together enough bodies to fulfil the fixture. The visitors brought 9 men 2 boys and, of course, their all important umpire; whilst Shappley gathered 10 men – plus umpire. Jim sat chewing his pencil, heart thumping with excitement, as Bill ambled up to the table with the magic words "Reckon yew'll 'efter play boy"; yet, even as he spoke, a new and unexpected face appeared – it was Stan, the younger brother of Big Wally, who had biked over from his home village with some kind of family message. Wally turned to Bill and asked – "Wot about Stan then Bill? E'll play if yer loike".

Stan, a big athletic young man, well known on football fields and other sporting events, but with little enthusiasm for 'Knockin' a ball about with a bit o' wood', was quite reluctant especially in view of his unsuitable garb – best blue Sunday double-breasted suit, collar and tie, and highly polished 'low ankle' shoes. Much to Jim's dismay, however, Stan gave in under pressure and agreed to 'make one'.

Batting first, Shappley were in dire straits with Seven Wickets down and only a miserable Twelve Runs to show for it when the makeshift Number 9 strode to the wicket – apparently without a care in the world, despite having his one and only pad tied precariously onto the wrong leg and having sartorially, done nothing more than remove his jacket. Disdaining guard he simply said "Ready when yew are", – and proceeded to slam the bowling in tremendous fashion – *not* in all directions, no, he used only the natural straight swing of the bat – smashing the ball back over the bowler time after time; five times the ball sailed high into the tops of the giant chestnut trees – to clatter down through the branches to the driveway below, six more bounced through the fence to keep Jim sufficiently busy so that his initial disappointment became overwhelmed and forgotten in all the excitement. The resident wood-pigeons which, 'man and boy', had for many summers, idly watched the play from their ideal vantage point high behind the bowler's arm, were most indignant at these continual intrusions into their normal summer Saturday afternoon siesta; as the missile hurtled towards them they took off in loud alarm and anger – then resettled for a bout of preening and grumbling, only to be brutally forced to become airborne again a few minutes later and thus allowed no real peace for nearly a whole hour. They failed to show up at the next match two weeks later – whether this absence was due to their own domestic arrangements, moulting, disgust, or simply self-preservation, only *they* would know.

The human spectators, fortunate enough to be present on that memorable day, remained in good voice and reasonably loyal – even if this mighty hitter was 'A bit of an outsider'. They had witnessed something never seen before and, almost certainly, would never be seen again. Bearing in mind that, normally, any batsman reaching double figures was likely to become the Village hero for at least a week – when an individual knock of a dozen or so equalled, in value, a Hammond century at Bristol or a Hobbs hundred at the Oval – what was the true value of this remarkable effort of *91*, out of 101 added during the time he was at the crease? The only innings this highly gifted young man ever played.

CHAPTER SEVENTEEN

The Domestic Scene

Purely by the whims of nature the Bates family suffered, in cricketing terms, 'a gap in the middle order', due to the fact that two girls were born after the first crop of boys and before the final Ralph and Jim. As was traditional and almost inevitable in those days, the girls – on leaving school were shunted off into 'Service' at whatever 'Big House' might be advertising a vacancy for parlour maid, kitchen maid, or any sort of female dogsbody. These unfortunate teenagers, therefore, were bundled out into the unknown world – clutching a pathetic parcel of personal belongings – to be deposited in some Mansion or Manor usually many miles from family, village, and friends – completely at the mercy of a number of strangers, not only the master and mistress themselves but also the incumbent heads of staff such as a Housekeeper or Butler. To all of whom she became the lowest of the low and often ended up as an ill-fed slave; but all that is another story, as they say.

The particular effect of this, however, in the Bates household was that the remaining males automatically fell into two separate age groups – with the older ones, by now deeply involved with the opposite sex – either courting or engaged. This situation threw the two youngest ones, Ralph and Jim, very much together whether they liked it or not. The difference in age and status became well epitomised at the meal table when, for example, on most Fridays, pork sausages took pride of place on the dinner plate. All those over twenty-one qualified for a whole sausage – whereas the lads had to share one between them. Mrs Bates was quite crafty here (as, indeed, she needed to be in all her culinary activities) by slicing the unfortunate fifth sausage nearly lengthwise so that, partly obscured by cabbage or gravy, each half

61

would appear quite normal and without signs of major surgery, thus any unexpected visitor would be misled, to some small degree, as to the dining family's means.

Likewise with the occasional treat of boiled eggs for Sunday breakfast because – although Mr Bates, like most villagers, kept as many as 40 or 50 chickens – his reasons were mainly to raise money rather than to augment the household menu. The eggs were carefully washed and graded so that, when the grocer delivered the weekly goods, he would return to his van loaded with a quantity of fresh eggs and reduce the bill accordingly. Sometimes, however, the hens slipped up and produced malformed, soft-shelled or cracked progeny which the grocer declined to accept; as with the sausages, the grown ups enjoyed a whole egg each whilst the 'young 'uns' shared one between them. In *this* case Mrs Bates displayed skill of the highest order in slicing a soft-boiled egg into two exactly equal halves and dropping them into the two waiting egg-cups without losing any yolk. Here again, the unexpected visitor would be most unlikely to notice or recognise the true facts.

On the all-important subject of cricket in general and batting in particular, the two teenagers, therefore, tended to discuss and speculate, between themselves, what their future in the game might hold in store.

Even so, the following season brought no great changes for Jim. He still did the scoring and on four occasions found himself in the team - twice officially selected and twice as a last minute stop-gap. He actually went to the crease only once and, after surviving three deliveries with reasonable competence, remained Nought Not-Out, so opportunities for experience or experiment were virtually nil. There were no opportunities for practice, of course, because the only possible venue was the little mown square out there in the middle and, even if George and Jack Bates – the groundsmen could have allowed the edges to be used for evening sessions – it was quite out of the question to dismantle all the fencing arrangement – then replace it again in semi-darkness.

Several years earlier, when Ralph and Jim were still at school, there were rumours of sports equipment being acquired – stumps, bats, pads and so on had been talked about – and *one* winter even mention of a real leather panelled football. It was thought that the reason nothing ever came of it was the opposition of parents who feared the adverse affect on the boy's school clothes – boots especially – so all experimenting and practice, by the young Bradman, must be done right there on the pitch with every one watching – including the 'Crowd' sitting on the old fallen elm.

Mrs Bates – a wonderful mother.

CHAPTER EIGHTEEN

A Match to Remember

Herewith the strange encounter with Cottam – the nearest and best known Village – being only a couple of miles away in the next Parish. This proximity produced a good deal of fraternising and inter-village marriages over the years, as a consequence the two sides usually included brother-in-law, cousins and workmates which resulted in a game that was also a social gathering.

No one has ever been able to find the reasons for the events on that particular Saturday in June 1935 (or was it '36). All the circumstances seemed normal – the weather good, with only a few woolly white clouds floating lazily around, nothing there to produce extra swing or any other abnormal help for the bowlers. The pitch? Average, prepared as usual by George and Jack; the outfield long and lush but no worse than usual.

Shappley, batting first, struck trouble immediately against the tall, rangy, left-arm-round, pace-man who opened from the drive end. Reg Owen played on from an inside edge in the first over. Phil Todd fell to a straight shooter. Jack Bates survived for only five balls before hearing his wickets rattle as well. Three good men gone and not yet a run on the board; and so the carnage went on – a run here and a run there but wickets falling at a sickening rate – indeed, a double figure total began to appear an over optimistic ambition. In the end, the Home side was completely humiliated by being dismissed for a disgraceful tally of Eleven Runs off Six and a Half Overs.

George summed up the situation in his usual down to earth but succinct manner – "Thass a roight bugger, thass what it is, a roight bugger, jist the time when we 'tickley wornted t' dew well tew", but he still sported a wide grin, as ever, regardless of the occasion or of the 'fag' paper hanging from his lower lip his fingers massaged the tobacco in readiness for the inevitable smoke before taking the field – because it was, of course, still well short of tea-time.

So the Shappley players gradually wandered out to the middle with little enthusiasm for the beating that awaited them. Alf bowled the first over from which two runs came – one for each batsman – and the formality was under way. Big Wally, at the other end, decided that under the hopeless circumstances, he too would try this 'Round-The-Wicket' lark and, much to everyone's astonishment, especially his own, removed three Cottam men in his first over!

"Ah well", remarked Charlie Booth, "thass something ennyway, losin' be seven wickets looks a soight better than a whoightwash".

Did Alf feel a trifle put out by this uppity 'Wally Stanton? certainly something seemed to give him new life after his rather lethargic first over. He tore in with a new sense of purpose and by the end of his six very unfriendly deliveries three more Cottam men had perished, two clean bowled and one caught behind. Six Wickets down for only Two Runs! The Shappley players heads were up again now, the adrenaline flowing and the cow-flies almost forgotten in this drama upon drama. Whilst any fiction writer would hesitate to pen the agonised writhing of the visiting batsmen – it has to be recorded that they found no answer to stop the history-making rot and succumbed completely for an almost unbelievable total of Three Runs. After the initial two singles in the first over no further runs came from the bat – the third being a scrambled bye when Bill Miller, standing two yards farther back than usual because of Alf's extra fire, lost the ball, momentarily, in the long grass.

Everyone walked off in a somewhat bemused and silent state of shock; George, of course, was first to recover – stating, to anyone who might be listening – "Well, I ain't never seen nuthin' loike that afore; no, that I never 'ev – an' sharn't never see nuthin loike it agin yew may depend on it".

The Cottam players, although shocked, were not terribly downhearted – after all, they *had* dismissed Shappley for that miserable score of eleven – a total which was abnormal but not unknown in local village records; indeed, between innings earlier, the men had exchanged reminiscences about "That time when 'Fendham' was shuvved out fer ten", or "When Netherby made only a dozen over there on their own dung 'eap".

The visiting Captain summed up their outlook best, perhaps, when he pointed out to Bill Miller that "It wuz a close old game Bill – yew only beat us be eight runs ar'ter all y' know".

Meanwhile young Jim struggled to get the scorebook tidied up and complete, with twenty wickets falling in about as mar.y overs he had been hard put to do any more than enter the bare essentials in his race to keep abreast of events and was only now beginning to recognise the true significance of the last last eighty minutes or so. After checking, yet again, the Cottam score – with its two singles at the top – followed by nine noughts, he sorted out the Shappley bowling figures, revealing that Alf had captured Six Wickets for Two Runs and, Big Wally Four for None.

As the weather remained good and the opposition happened to be Cottam – a 'Beer-Match' after tea was agreed upon – so that a full afternoon's play might still be enjoyed by all – including the cows who led Jim a merry dance, during the never-ending tea interval, with their usual attack on the playing area. One skittish young heifer seemed exceptionally persistent and more intent, apparently on causing trouble than in tasting this choice patch of grass. However, the small, lone defender managed to keep his patch reasonably undamaged until the long hour was up and the men returned, at which, the animals recognised defeat and reluctantly retired to deep extra cover to chew the cud and, no doubt, look forward to a resumption of activities in two weeks' time.

The 'Beer Match' was taken quite literally, in that both teams repaired to the 'Dog And Duck' for the evening where the losers supplied the first gallon of Best Bitter. Then the Cottam men avowed they could, and would, 'Wipe the floor' with the Home Team on the dartboard. This assertion must surely have been engendered more by alcoholic fumes than by commonsense – because any darts team which included Phil Owen could hardly be looked upon as beatable by throwers of ordinary mortal standing. It should here be noted that his mathematics, whilst in action, were equally as fast and accurate as the 'Arrers he propelled into almost any double or treble that happened to attract his attention. How this numerical expertise married up with his trades as a Thatcher-Cum-Chimneysweep-Cum-Animal Slaughterer is difficult to see.

Thus, eventually, these cheerful invaders from Cottam drifted out into the darkness, mounted their bikes and prepared for home; a mixture of laughs and curses emanated from the front yard as the inevitable problems arose in lighting up the temperamental 'Bacon-Friers' and someone discovering he had a flat back tyre. Worst of all was the plight of Ben, a large amiable bear of a man, whose bike could not be found. The Landlord, when acquainted with this rare and unfortunate situation, emerged from the bar-room bearing aloft the big brass paraffin lamp, which normally hung, and smoked, over the Domino Table, and made another search which gradually widened into the road and nearby hedges with some thirty or more men now involved. Suddenly a voice shouted "Whassat on the sign-post?" and sure enough, the lamplight revealed Ben's bike hanging peacefully, if somewhat precariously, eight feet up on the sign bearing, ironically, the words 'Cottam 2¼ miles'.

It required all the strength and skill of a smallish man, standing on Ben's broad shoulders, to gradually ease the machine safely off its perch and two more to lower it to the ground. Being the man he was – Ben laughed louder than anyone at the ingenuity of some person or persons unknown. All the Shappley men had been outside from time to time during the evening for obvious reasons so there was no way he could know who to accuse of the dastardly deed, but, no doubt, a mental note had been made for appropriate retaliation of some kind when Shappley next visited Cottam!

After the many 'Cheerio's' And 'Goodnoights' were over the visitors disappeared down the lane in merry mood – their humiliating experience of the afternoon temporarily forgotten; whilst the local lads drifted off in ones and twos – also content with a day well spent, especially George and Jack – the former wondering if 'a drop of paraffin' would remove the smear of bikechain oil marks from his right hand and, the latter hoping the dusty tyre marks on the shoulder of his best jacket would not leave any permanent stains. Fortunately for them both – these blemishes had been hidden from Ben's sight by the friendly June darkness.

The site of the missing bicycle. (Photograph from Hertfordshire Countryside magazine, used with permission.)

CHAPTER NINEEEN

The Cricket Season

The cricket season was far too short for our embryo runmaker. He dreamed of a climate that would allow, at least, ten months of fine warm weather – or else a society so arranged that cricket might be played, by those who so wished, for six days a week during the existing English summer. The harsh facts of reality, however meant that only some fifty or sixty hours of play were possible in a whole year! The reasons for this miserably small ration were many and due, in the main, to the way of life customary at that time and place.

In the first place, most of the cricketers were, almost of necessity, also members of the football team; consequently the summer game must await the conclusion of its winter counterpart. The 'whites' would therefore emerge from their moth-balls at about the middle of May. At the end of the season the same problem arose in reverse, as football always had to take preference, thus early September saw the big ball once again take over from the small.

Secondly, there could be no such thing as *Sunday* cricket, so that, even with the inclusion of Whit-Monday and August Bank Holiday Monday, the Fixture Card would reveal, at most, twenty matches in store; of these, two or three might be lost through rain and possibly one or two more when hay-time and harvest demanded man power whenever the crops and weather were right – regardless of what day of the week it might be. So an average season might produce only 16 or 17 games.

Furthermore, most matches didn't really get underway until around 3.30 despite the 2.30 religiously shown on all fixture cards and team sheets. Also, with tea being very much a social and lengthy affair – usually in a local pub or village hall – an hour could quite easily slip away, leaving something like three hours actual playing time for the day. This dearth of opportunity, plus the difficult conditions most of the time, may be easily seen when, at the end of the season, Jim struggled to work out the individual Averages from the scorebook; a typical example might show Charlie Booth top of the batting with:-

Innings	Not Out	Aggregate	Average
15	1	126	9

The rest would make do with averages of 8 down to the 'Depths'. The bowling, however, was quite a different story whereby, in the same number of matches in a season, individuals like Alf Marsh and 'Big Wally' returned figures which would have been the envy of Larwood, Voce, or Verity – Alf 65 Wickets at 3.5 in less than 200 overs and Wally 59 Wickets at 3.9 in even fewer overs. It was within this daunting framework of figures that our ambitious young village lad began to see something of the mountain to be climbed.

Guesting for Westford Cricket Club. The author pictured at beginning of front row.

CHAPTER TWENTY

Ups and Downs

The winter of 1936-7 round young Jim thinking seriously about changing his job – for health reasons. Plainly his sporting ambitions would be severely handicapped if he was weak and unfit. The small local iron-foundry where he had spent nearly two years, since leaving school, was old, dark and very dirty. Each evening he arrived home as black as a typical coalminer. His working overalls were discarded immediately inside the scullery door to avoid contaminating the rest of the house and furniture with the all pervading black sand in which he worked all day. Worse still, he realised, was the fine black dust he must be continually inhaling and causing all sorts of lasting damage. Feeding the smelting furnace was his most dreaded job – twice a week this roaring monster was brought to fiery life to melt down the scrap-iron to a fearsome white hot liquid which was then transformed into thousands of new ploughshares and other cast iron agricultural requirements.

Many barrow loads of coke had to be wheeled from across the road just to get the voracious creature hot enough to even *consider* its main diet of old scrap machinery which must first be smashed to pieces with sledge hammers to make digestion quicker and easier.

Four feet in diameter and ten feet high this clay lined steel cylinder – made hideous by the roaring high speed blast fan – was a frightening thing for *anyone* to feed let alone a six-stone lad. As Jim climbed the ladder propped against the furnace flank with a container of scrap-iron balanced on his head – gobbets of liquid iron fell like hailstones on and around him. They were blown up and out of the furnace's innards by the tremendous force of the blast fan. His clothes were riddled with small black edged holes and each time he came down the ladder it was necessary to make a hurried search to remove pellets which might burn right through to the skin. So up and down he went – every five minutes or so – tipping one container of coke and one of iron into the white-hot jaw of this insatiable monster.

Although his new job involved more travelling each day and accepting a lower wage – Jim reckoned the healthier environment of the small brewery made it well worth while. Father Bates vetoed the move most emphatically at first because of the reduction in household income of one-and-sixpence a week, on reflection however, the thought of fewer Doctor's bills changed his mind – with seven shillings and sixpence a visit and all medicines or treatment to be paid for – this became an important factor. The following spring revealed a bigger and healthier young man taking his place in the Cricket Club as a recognised player. Phil Todd, the Thatcher-cum-Chimney Sweep, had moved away 'to pastures new', so a vacancy appeared in the regular eleven. A new scorer was trained and all looked set fair for the great break-through by the confident young Number eleven – but, it was not to be; Jim's ambitions received a nasty setback and his resolutions were badly shaken by a season's tally of 14 Runs in 12 Innings, Seven Times Not-Out, Highest Score – Three! A sad blow indeed but the fires of ambition refused to be quenched; 'If big successes fail to appear', his voice of conscience reminded him, 'then more satisfaction must be realised and enjoyed from the occasional small ones' – such as the catch held in the field or the defensive batting for several overs which sometimes enabled a partner to add a few more valuable runs.

In contrast to Jim's lack of batting success, his elder brother Jack set a new batting record for the Club by carrying his bat throughout the innings of 97 for a personal 50 Not-Out. This was on one of the rare occasions when Shappley enjoyed the delights of playing on a *real* cricket ground – with a mown outfield and not a bullock in sight. Some wiseacre insisted he remembered "Old Tom, wot got killed in the War, knockin' up Fifty Tew afore 'e wos Run-Out, over at Great Dunton; 'bout Nineteen Twelve or Thutteen I reckon it wos". Whilst another brought to mind Old Sam what used ter keep the 'Dog and Duck', 'e carried 'is bat once fer 38 Not-Out down 'ere on our own dung-'eap". Nevertheless, both agreed that "Nobody 'ad ever scored fifty *and* carried 'is bat roight threw an innins".

Strange to relate, on this delightful ground – much in favour of batting – the home side fell for only 23 Runs – completely destroyed by the whippy accuracy of young Alf with figures of 9 Wickets for 11 Runs – 7 clean bowled. Incidentally, this bowling performance by Alf was quickly proved to be no flash-in-the-pan when, the very next week, he captured 6 Wickets for 5 Runs – 5 clean bowled – in a match which saw the opposition all out for 16 in only 11 Overs. An astonishing 9 for 5 in a later match helps to explain his overall figures, that season, of 78 Wickets at a cost of less than Four Apiece!

CHAPTER TWENTY-ONE

Mecca

As had happened several times before, the young hopeful's resolutions were to be buttressed by the unexpected. Just at the time when things looked at their bleakest there came an event which was, perhaps, the most important in Jim's cricket ambitions. Out of the blue, he was invited to join his three elder brothers on a trip to that fabulous place called 'Lords'. *They* had been once before, during the previous summer; how they all managed to inveigle a day off from work was a mystery never explained or mentioned.

In a dreamworld of anticipation – not daring to get too deeply excited, in case rain or some other problem should destroy the whole project, Jim sweated out the remaining week or two of waiting.

On the appointed day, however, all were up at 5.30 a.m. to see a sky full of promise. Sandwiches were prepared, bottles of cold tea for George and Jack – artificial lemonade for the younger ones. The journey began with a 7-mile bike ride to Barford (the nearest railway station), fairly humdrum so far but from then on young Jim was in a daze – he simply followed the others blindly onto platforms, up steps and down steps, on trains and off trains, above ground and deep into frightening underground caverns awash with people and noise; until, suddenly, it seemed, there before his very eyes lay the vast expanse of immaculate lawn, surrounded by thousands of people in shirt sleeves or summer dresses settling into their seats for the day. Even as he was still trying, goggle-eyed to take all this in, a rattle of applause sounded from all around the ground as the 'Gladiators entered the Arena'. George said " 'Ullo, the're goona make a start then"; adding, "Yearse, yew may depend on it the're ready fer orf". To which Jack observed that "Neither umpire looks loike Joe", whilst Ralph rustled around with his cushion, vitals, scorecard, and various other bits and pieces like a farmyard hen preparing a nest. Jim tried to watch everything at once – half afraid to blink for fear of missing something.

The first significant fact he noted about the eleven players now running down the pavilion steps onto the 'lawn' was that all were dressed completely in creamy white from the neck down. A smattering of coloured caps – but no braces, no brown or grey trousers and everyone wearing white cricket boots – even the two Umpires

Another ripple of applause heralded the appearance of the opening batsmen – again, immaculately turned out with all the correct protective gear well in evidence – except, of course, the hidden, 'not-to-be-talked-of' box.

The opening bowler ominously, tossing the bright red (new?) ball idly from hand to hand, appeared to be on his way to speak to a friend in the crowd but stopped about half-way – made a mark on the ground, then turned and loped in towards the wickets – increasing speed with every stride and flung over his arm as he reached the Umpire – the batsman moved his right foot back and across to the offside – holding his bat high in the air – then came a smacking sound as the wicket-keeper, some 20 yards back, seemed to catch something; 'All very well', thought Jim 'All very elegant and nice to watch this going through the motions', I suppose, 'But let's get on with it *properly* and start using the ball'. Once more the same ritual unfolded and Jim wondered how long this rehearsal business was to continue – then he heard brother George remark, with obvious admiration, "I'm sure 'e ee'nt tuckin' 'em down there none. I ee'nt seen the ball at *all* yet!" From which, poor Jim realised that he must watch more closely if he was to enjoy this spectacle to the full. He'd never imagined it possible that bowling could be so fast that spectators might have difficulty in seeing the ball's passage from bowler to batsman and wicket-keeper. The next two deliveries were met by the bat with that beautiful sound that only true cricketers can fully appreciate – one turned neatly down to long leg for Two Runs and the next played solidly back to the bowler. From then on Jim quickly got his sight focussing properly and began to see the flash of red as the fast bowlers let fly; 'But', he pondered, 'How on earth does the batsman see it in time to make his decisions and appropriate movements?' Obviously the day was going to be an eye-opener in more ways than one and the purpose of the many pairs of binoculars to be seen amongst the crowd now became clear. The Shappley Number Eleven decided there and then that, on the evidence provided so far, he was not yet quite ready to open the batting for England.

As the overs passed and runs were scored his attention was drawn to the extraordinary score board which, with so many things to watch and absorb, had so far escaped his notice; Intrigued by it though he was, however, its full investigation must wait until dinner time rather than miss any of the goings on out there in the middle.

So rivetted was his attention on the play that the various noises, talk, and activities going on around him didn't really register – he failed, completely, to hear George's question of "D'yer wornt a droppa cold tea Jim?" an offer which, after being repeated twice without response, was withdrawn until the temporarily deaf young lad came back to normal.

Dinner time came as something of a shock to the avid watcher – so absorbed was he in the completely new experience. When the umpires lifted the bails and the players all trooped off – some spectators began to stand up and stroll around to ease aching bones, no doubt. Others were digging into their boxes and bags for sandwiches and other necessities of life – so he, too, joined in this time of relaxation which allowed an opportunity to listen to the various conversations going on around him from which he learned a great deal about the players, the match, and many other issues concerning professional cricket. The positioning of the fielders, for example, was apparently of great importance here, whereas back at Shappley, and elsewhere, only two or three men were put in specific positions near the wicket – the rest spread themselves around the outfield in a rough circle. This was not due necessarily to a lack of cricket know-how but more for practical reasons – first, because it was impossible to judge, on such pitches, where the batsman may be likely to hit the ball, and secondly, it made sense to cover as wide an area as possible so as to be better able to spot where the ball landed and thus have a better chance of finding quickly.

He learned, too, the purpose of the two strange white boards at each end of the ground which were moved this way or that from time to time during play. He also found that, possibly because of their one or two previous visits, George and Jack were much more knowledgeable about the first-class game than he had realised, so Jim took the opportunity to pester them with questions as to "Why did the Wicket-keeper do this?" and, "Why did the Non-Striker do that?" Why did the Bowler change to round The Wicket?" or, "Why were there some times four men in the Slips and sometimes only *one* – or *none*?" until, eventually, Jack warned him "You'd better git on with y' dinner afore they come out agin". He found this advice to be eminently sound and acceptable so with due care in saving one jam sandwich, one half-slice of plain cake and two inches of lemonade in the bottle, for the tea interval – he quickly dealt with the rest well before play re-started.

George, meantime, had struck up a rather unlikely conversation with a bowler-hatted 'Gentleman of the City' – probably a stockbroker or Foreign Office type pinching the afternoon off. Strange though it may seem they both appeared to be enjoying the experience – even without the services of an interpreter! Possibly George's habit of saying everything over a second time helped to overcome the language problem.

The 'Bowler Hat' *did*, however, decline most politely, but emphatically, to accept a lump of the countryman's real cheddar – perhaps he was simply not hungry, or possibly a trifle suspicious of the large left thumb entrapping the cheese onto its bread foundation. It might even have been the fierce looking in-curved pruning knife used in the dismembering that affected his appetite! – his instincts warning him, no doubt, that this same weapon was used for many other purposes, in its normal daily life, beyond that of hacking lumps of bread and cheese.

Back to young Jim and the match with the monstrous scoreboard now showing '102 for No Wicket' – this in itself gave him much to marvel at – for two hours various bowlers had flung, hurled, twisted and twirled the ball with all their skill and strength at the two opening batsmen without success; they must, indeed, be something more than human, the lad decided, as they settled in again – intent, it seemed, on continuing throughout the afternoon session. Then at that very moment, there came a loud and concerted appeal from the fielders and the batsman, who'd just passed his 50, turned and made his way to the pavilion amidst great applause. The successful bowler happened to be the very fast opener with the extra long run-up so Jim hadn't seen exactly what happened but the wicket-keeper was joyfully tossing the ball high so a fine nick off the edge of the bat seemed most likely – but just to make sure, before filling in his scorecard

Jim questioned Ralph, equally as absorbed in every detail – "Caught Behind", he replied rather shortly, plainly not wishing to be distracted at that particular moment when his whole attention was centred on the Wicket-keeper – whose activities had, of course, been his main attraction since the match started.

Jim continued to concentrate on the batsmen, studying mainly their footwork which he'd instinctively grasped as the secret of their remarkable skills. He tried to memorise, for future use, *where* exactly those swift-moving white boots went as the ball came hurtling down – and, just as important, *when* the moves were made. Even from his square-leg viewpoint in the stands it was quite plain that, generally, they moved *into* the line of the ball – mostly forward as well – but occasionally back if the delivery pitched short. After spending a complete half-hour watching the batsman's head only it became clear, to the young man's straining eyes, that foot and head moved, usually, in unison to that all important line.

And so, the afternoon rolled on, wickets fell and many runs were scored – a little more freely now – and every minute brought new and exciting examples of skill for Jim to marvel at – the strokes so sure and controlled, the calling and running between wickets so sharp and decisive – despite the wonderful bowling and fielding; plus, of course, the efficiency and apparent nonchalance of Ralph's particular hero behind the Stumps whether standing a whole pitches length back to the fast men or up close, with the peak of his cap hovering over the bails, to the spinners.

Tea-time came and went, as did the remains of the 'vitals'. For some obscure reason Jack and George had changed seats and now the former was deep in conversation with the 'City Gent'; as far as Jim could make out, during the tea interval, the subject now under discussion, between these representatives of town and country, was the technique of rolling home-made cigarettes! The 'C.G.' was obviously quite baffled as to how those thick knobbly fingers of Jack's could manufacture, in seconds, a reasonable looking cigarette. The whole operation, from start to finish, demanded extreme delicacy of touch – more suited, surely, to his own slender well manicured hands – yet, when he accepted Jack's offer "Ere, 'ev a goo y'self", he was much too clumsy and fumble-fingered, still it was no doubt an experience worth recounting to his friends on the Stock Exchange, or wherever, tomorrow – indeed, his whole day would be remembered as one new adventure.

As the evening wore on and close of play began to loom up, Jim's headache worsened – simply through the hours of constant staring and concentrating – but he still dreaded the arrival of 6.30 when all these white-clad demi-gods would disappear from view. Nevertheless, it had to come, eventually, and it was time to leave the dreamland and join the chattering throng surging out through the gates.

The journey home failed to register on his tired young brain at all – he merely followed his elders obediently and silently with his head packed with many wonders and a thousand things to remember for the future, for there could no longer be the slightest doubt which batting methods to follow, after the six solid hours demonstrated before his own eyes this long and memorable day.

The only snag of the day occurred when the four cricketers left the train at the now dark and deserted Home Station and retrieved their bikes to pedal the final seven miles back to Clome. Jim's 'Baconfriar' refused to function – three times he lit the tiny wick but each time the flame withered and died almost as quick as the matches themselves. "Cummorn Jim", shouted Jack, "Git a move on, I gotta be up at ar' past five in the mornin' ", then came back to ooo what the hold up was – his first words were, as usual, straight to the point – "Ez it got plenty of paraffin in?" and Jim had to mumblingly confess that, in all the excitement of the early morning departure, he had, indeed, forgotten to fill his lamp. Fortunately, for him the holiday spirit still lingered and he suffered no serious recriminations – only a gruff "Keep close be'ind us all the time, an' if the 'Bobby' stops us, leave the talking t'me". So they pedalled off along the dark country road – slowed down, as usual, by George's habitual 'second-gear' outlook on life and the general axiom of 'Never doing to-day what you can leave 'til tomorrow'. The little convoy did, in fact meet the village constable on his nightly 'anti-poacher' rounds (also on a bike of course); apparently, however his view of three bobbing lights approaching confused his judgement as to exactly how many shadowy bodies were attached. Possibly he was influenced to some extent, by George's cheery "Noice noight, Ted!" as they passed like ships in the night.

After expressing his appreciation to his brothers for giving him such a marvellous day Jim shakily lit the candle, staggered upstairs to bed and, surprisingly perhaps, slept solidly all night.

CHAPTER TWENTY-TWO

Oddley End

A new fixture for Shappley to contend with was Oddley End. a sprawling type village reached only after a long and wearisome bike ride of some five or six miles which seemed to be up-hill most of the way. Having arrived eventually in a hot and fairly breathless condition, the team learned, from a tobacco-chewing local, that the cricket pitch "Lay acrorse them fields mate", – to which there was neither road nor pathway, consequently bikes and the club-bag were manhandled over several fences and stiles. Nevertheless, once discovered it proved to be its own reward; surrounded on three sides by trees and high hedges – with a view of the Church and 'Olde Worlde' village on the other – it enjoyed all the aspects of picture postcard England; furthermore, to the visitor's delight, the 'official' residents of the field were thirty or forty friendly looking sheep which meant that most of the fielding difficulties were swept away in one stroke – fewer flies, no mess (other than a few harmless 'currants') and above all, an outfield uniformly close cropped all over – short enough for the ball to be in full view at all times – so fielding would be a great pleasure in itself.

Ralph, had, by now, become safely settled in his coveted position behind the stumps, so much so that he'd found it possible to shift some concentration back to batting again, with considerable success. Jim was both pleased and envious at this development. Pleased, for obvious reasons, as twenties and thirties came from Ralph's bat from time to time – especially as he was of similar mind in trying to follow the lead demonstrated by bruised but unbowed Schoolmaster. Evidence and events indicated that both Bates boys were on much the same track and this fact alone gave Jim some satisfaction and moral support to stick to his guns despite his continued failures. At the same time, it was sometimes difficult to prevent an element of envy creeping in as he watched his brother's left foot down the wicket approach bringing the results that *he* so desperately desired.

Back to Oddley End where the Home Team is batting - Five wickets were down for 60 odd – probably about 'par for the course' under the rather more pleasant conditions. Number Seven reached the Crease – Jim was fielding in his usual spot at Silly Mid-On and was fascinated by the man's sartorial splendour' – beginning with highly polished brown brogues – those with little round holes punched into the leather in various patterns, nice white trousers tucked carefully into navy blue socks before attaching the pads. The trousers swelled out on the way up to accommodate a large posterior and ample waist – at which, point they were encompassed, rather than supported, by a gleaming black wide leather belt bearing a bright brass buckle. *Real* support for the trousers was most efficiently supplied by a dashing pair of braces – two inches wide and rich Raw Umber in colour. The shirt was impeccably white with sleeves rolled high up to the shoulders revealing biceps of ominous size — in keeping with massive forearms of a reddish mahogany colour liberally covered with gingery hair. All this elegance was topped by a flat cap of a brown tweedy mixture and apparently brand new. 'Plainly a man who loves his cricket', Jim thought, 'A man who works hard probably on the land with horses and, although not very good at the game, is so enthusiastic about it that he views appearance as being of high importance'.

The extra desires of both Ralph and Jim to learn everything they could about the game – especially after that never-to-be-forgotten day at Lords last year – had led to understanding why a batsman may sometimes be put off by someone or something passing behind the bowler's arm as he is about to deliver; in village cricket, however, the problem was scarcely ever thought about or even recognised. When our enthusiastic Number Seven of Oddley End was ready to face up to his first ball – Ralph held up a restraining gloved hand to the bowler and inquires of the batsman "Is that old chap ambling along by the hedge behind the bowler going to bother you" Flat Cap's eyes followed the pointing glove and replied "Oh no, 'e'll be safe 'anuff, I never 'its 'em straight, I all'us 'it 'em over to that way", and waved a nonchalant arm in the vague direction of Long-on.

CHAPTER TWENTY-THREE

Brother Against Brother

Each season, for many years, had been rounded off, on the last Saturday before football took over, with a special match within the Village. A match which brought brother against brother and, sometimes, father against son. It came about when, one day in the past, the Squire claimed he could raise a side from his Estate good enough to beat the rest of the Parish. No idle boast this, bearing in mind his many employees plus four cricketing sons.

This event became an immediate success from the moment of its inception and was much looked forward to by all concerned – indeed, on one occasion, when the weather co-operated extra well, a crowd of *seventeen* adults and numerous children watched the play.

Naturally, young Jim was most excited about it – despite the constantly intruding thought that it signalled the end of cricket for the next seven or eight months. He felt confident that this year would find him officially selected for the Shappley team for the first time in this match and as the demands of the 'Squire's XI robbed the Village of several regular batsmen Jim could reasonably hope to be fairly well up the order.

So the Estate team, with Fred Owen the Gamekeeper, Jack Bates and Bob Green from the Garden Staff, Tom Green the Ostler, the four young Squires with a guest or two, perhaps, all down from Cambridge – had to be looked upon as formidable; although, over the years, the results had more or less evened out.

Apart from the special pleasure and challenge of competing against one's own team-mates there was the added, and perhaps even *more* important, joy of playing in a completely different atmosphere than that experienced in many of the standard fixtures. Here, for instance, the Umpires were entirely un-partisan and usually appeared reluctant to give *any*body out. It was fortunate, of course, that Bob and Tom Green, by virtue of their employment, ended up on the same side; had they, perchance, been in opposition the whole match might well have turned into a three or four hour argument – rising and falling, perhaps, in intensity but never really ceasing

The statistics of the match in general turned out to be fairly average – the Estate XI Fifty six All Out – due mostly to a fine 21 by the Bugatti owner and a reply of Forty Seven by the Village. Important to Jim, however, was his exalted position at Number 5 where, with Ralph, a stand of 27 was established – putting the team well in line for a surprise win after a rather poor start – but, it was not to be. The somewhat inexperienced tail folded rather quickly. Being second top scorer with 8 after Ralph's 15 gave Jim something pleasant to help the winter through – especially as Four of them came in one blow, to square leg, off brother Jack.

CHAPTER TWENTY-FOUR

Stirrings of Optimism

Despite the infusion of knowledge and enthusiasm provided by that glorious day at Lords watching the top-level players – the next season again proved disappointing to the young hopeful. He was, of course, still committed completely to the Game in all its aspects and, fortunately, his battered ego received an occasional dab of 'soothing ointment' – mainly due once again to the efforts of the ubiquitous Mr White, whose various official positions in the Club naturally included that of Fixture Secretary. In this capacity he had, for some time, been beavering away, by letter and by personal contacts, to obtain fixtures for Shappley with some of the big establishments in Town such as schools, factories, and the hospital, all of which had their own proper cricket fields with short mown grass right to the boundary edge, a pavilion and various other luxuries plus a noticeable and extremely welcome absence of cows and their special breed of flies. Whilst the good man *may* have been urged on by just a 'teeny' thought in connection with his own batting style, (which must surely prosper on these better grounds and better pitches) his main aim, without doubt, was to provide facilities whereby the whole team's standards might improve and, at the same time, allow everyone to enjoy fielding and batting, in particular, under such delightful conditions. Where the ball could be kept in sight at all times, chased and picked up without any natural hazard or hindrances. For the time being, these well-blessed clubs could offer only the odd evening match because their Saturdays, naturally enough, were fully booked. These altruistic efforts by Mr White, however, brought their own problems for some of the Shappley players – several of whom worked until 5.30 in the evening and, with only one small car available, it would be impossible for anyone to bike the seven miles to Barford in time for a Six, or even Six-thirty, start. These difficulties became, in fact, beneficial to Jim and Ralph whose place of work was on the way to Town, anyway, so by taking one or two extra items of clothing with them to work in the morning they were always able to participate, and, in the weakened sides, Jim often found himself well up the batting order above the budding younger boys who had to be drafted in to make up the number.

The indefatigable Hampshire man, would somehow manage to scrape a side together and chivvy it to the required place at roughly the required time.

The first of these matches took place at the Hospital ground – where Jim made a pleasant enough Twelve Not-Out, batting at Number Seven. How many he might have scored, had the Captain not declared, can only be guessed at but he was free to dream!

The third and last of these extra evening treats of the season brought the Villagers to the Town Grammar School where, with harvest-time adding to the problems of team 'collection', Ralph and Jim were flung in at the deep end to open the innings and were fortunate enough, on a good pitch, to first survive, then enjoy, an opening stand of 78 Runs, an achievement which later sent people searching their memories and past scorebooks to find out when, if ever, such a thing had been done before! The new young Jack Hobbs share of 28 Runs, including four boundaries, was easily his highest and best yet and, naturally, extremely satisfying but, it must be said that the Grammar School side was also below strength for some reason and included several lads in Jim's age group.

So these excursions did much to keep his pecker up as he struggled during the Saturday matches. It also meant that Captain/Schoolmaster White and others were persuaded to persevere with his selection – and not necessarily as Number Eleven! Apparently the general view, he gathered from chance remarks, was that he always *looked* like making runs! 'How many striving batsmen have carried that tag one wonders sometimes throughout a whole cricketing life-time?

So, at last, things might be said to be looking up; a few runs were coming here and there but generally only on the better grounds. He desperately needed a good knock on the Home Ground – if only to appease the elderly critics who regularly watched and commented from their fallen dead tree grandstand.

CHAPTER TWENTY-FIVE

'The Day of Reckoning'

The coming of spring may mean many different things to different people – May blossom and daffodils, perhaps, to some, or grass-cutting and seed-sowing to others. To Jim, however, it heralded only one thing – the start of a new Cricket Season in which all kinds of exciting events may take place. The past winter had been a little less difficult than usual due to the slight financial improvements in the Bates' household. Probably the two most important items, resulting from this relative affluence being, firstly, his acquisition of a pair of real cricket trousers and boots. Secondly, the appearance in the living-room, of a wireless set. The latter device was not the boon it *might* have been because Mr Bates decreed it must only be used for 'The News' and Church Services. Naturally it was enjoyed for many other things when he was well away off the premises – although a watch had to be kept against his possible unexpected return. So it was then, that Howard Marshall became an occasional, but extremely important, verbal visitor with his Test-match broadcasts.

The inhabitants of Shappley Parish, as a whole, were not quite sure whence the Squire's great wealth came; that he was, in some way, involved with the manufacture of footwear became evident each Christmas when all his outdoor staff received a new pair of boots, of their choice, as a gift. The connection was further strengthened during the cricket season when Shappley enjoyed an annual fixture with a team from a big London leather factory with which he was obviously concerned.

For some years, since its inauguration, this match had taken place at Shappley on August Bank Holiday Monday – allowing an 11.30 start – two innings each side. This arrangement provided a great day out in the country for the London cricketers and their families. The charabanc would thread its hesitant way through the narrow leafy lanes of Barfordshire to arrive at the Village at about 10.30 and disgorge its excited passengers into this strange world of huge trees, hedges and grass. Real cows lazily scratching themselves against the wire fence around the cricket table and fighting their unending battle against the relentless flies.

The visitors brought their own midday 'vittals' of sandwiches, cakes and lemonade. Tea, of course, was taken in the Village Hall as usual and proved quite a social affair – with speeches and various extra dainties. The ladies and children, in particular, found much to interest them in such items as the locally baked bread – specially delivered that very afternoon – and the dairy produce of milk, butter and cream – all straight from the hoof. Obviously, therefore, this was a day looked forward to by all concerned, especially as the cricket itself was devoid of the frequent personality clashes and animosity all too often seen in the normal local fixtures. The London cricketers' annual visit was, to some extent, a practical necessity because the factory possessed no sports facilities of its own. Consequently the Shappley ground, with its many drawbacks, had hitherto been the only option. *This* year, however, the Squire announced, early in the season, that the custom would be changed. Apparently his considerable influence 'In Town' enabled him to acquire the use of a cricket ground somewhere in London so the whole process, this year, would be carried out in reverse.

So, on that warm Monday morning in early August, Mrs Bates rose earlier than usual to prepare three parcels of food, one bottle of cold tea and two of ersatz lemonade, for Jack, Ralph and Jim. George, now married, would be 'vitalled up' by his wife. Most of the passengers on the charabanc, which left at 9 a.m., had never been to London before and, with no television or films available, had little idea of what lay before them so speculation as to what they might see and experience during the ensuing twelve hours provided ample conversation on the journey.

As the strange looking scenery unfolded some of the wide-eyed travellers began to feel as if they were entering a foreign country. After a brief stop at the leather factory, to pick up one of the home cricketers as a guide, the driver steered his careful way through a bewildering maze of streets – each one carrying more vehicles than might be seen around Shappley in a lifetime. Suddenly there came a break, in the seemingly endless miles of buildings, to reveal a wide open space of rather odd-looking fields, fields where all the grass had been shorn uniformly short – like huge lawns – with not a cow, horse, or sheep in any of them! This must, indeed, be a foreign country, and rich too, if grassy meadows could be kept solely for sport. The several fields, each separated by low, white wooden fences, boasted its own pavilion in which the visitors soon discovered they might change and store their dinner parcels. George opined to everybody in general that "It must be 'andy when it rains tew, yearse, bit better'n th' ole 'olly bush eh?" Ralph and Jim, having no 'fag' rolling to do, set off immediately to explore this wonderland; whilst both had played in a few 'shortgrass' matches they hadn't seen anything as grand as this. After a good look at the well-prepared pitch they wandered over to inspect the sight-screens – the purpose of which was, of course, no longer a mystery to the Bates family younger section. Although they were much smaller and less elaborate than those seen last year at Lords, they were, nevertheless, quite impressive from touching distance.

Activity of various kinds was bringing the whole area to life. On adjoining pitches stumps were being positioned, sight-screens pushed around and, here and there white clad figures knocking balls about – giving a general air of excitement and expectancy – or, at least, that's how it affected young Jim who felt he'd already experienced as much as he could stand for one day – yet there was still a whole day's cricket to come – including the possibility of two visits to the crease and fielding on this delightful sward.

Due to the usual demands of the harvest fields the Shappley team looked sadly weakened, the batting line-up being minus Fred Owen, the solid Game-keeper-cum-opener who might well have revelled in these conditions but, there it was – he must leave his pheasants temporarily and become a farm-worker. Charlie Booth and the argumentative Green Brothers were also roped in for this all important work. By pure good fortune one of these gaps was being filled by one of the Squire's sons who happened to be available and, as we have seen, a very useful cricketer. It was also comforting, to some extent, that the remaining six and a half regulars (Jim being the half!) included several all-rounders – an important factor, indeed, bearing in mind the crippling absence of both Alf and Big Wally who for several seasons had, between them, captured ninety per cent of the total wickets taken by the team. The rest of the side was made up with young lads with little pretence of cricket ability but intent, mainly, on a good day out.

Having won the toss and, for reasons known only to himself, Mr White invites the home side to take first knock; at ten minutes to noon Jack Bates bowls the first over, in his enforced promotion as the spearhead of the attack, and is immediately rewarded with a wicket. Phil Todd turns his arm over with half-a-dozen fairly friendly deliveries and the match is well and truly under way.

Despite this early success the countrymen are fully expecting to be leather chasing for an unusually long time – bearing in mind the excellent batting conditions and the paucity of front line bowlers; nevertheless, such is the extra pleasure of fielding on the delightful smooth turf – plus the near absence of flies – the prospect brings pleasant anticipation rather than foreboding.

Much to everyone's surprise, however, all speculations are proved wrong because Jack's friendly paced swing bowling scythes through the batting with such effect that they muster a total of only 36 All Out! with stand-in Jack Bates taking 8 Wickets for 9 Runs in only 6 Overs! This exceptional performance means that with only about half the normal batting strength available Shappley ought to sneak a first innings lead.

As the time is still short of one o'clock – George suggests "We moight as well make a start afore dinner a'nt we? yearse, moight as well git a few on the board afore dinner if we can, I reckon". Most of the seniors nod in agreement as they concentrate, partly, on the important ritual of methodically constructing a home-made cigarette. Jim had often wondered about this strange ceremony that took place, it seemed, during every break in a match. Whilst there were one or two confirmed pipemen, one who chewed plug tobacco and a couple of non-smokers – the majority 'rolled their own' and he found it quite fascinating to watch half-a-dozen brawny men, with big clumsy looking fingers, engaged in this extremely delicate operation. Conversation usually continued unhindered despite the close concentration required and the flimsy 'fag paper' hanging precariously from each lower lip. Eventually, after a final roll and deft sliding lick of the tongue the job was done and ignition applied; battered tins snapped shut and returned to jacket pockets – always the *left*-hand pocket, he noticed, and wondered why.

Back to The Day Of Reckoning! Mr White decides to promote himself to open the innings – thinking, no doubt, that under these batting conditions he, with his left foot forward – head over the ball approach, is likely to succeed; he should gather a much richer reward, today, for his deft glances, cuts and firm pushes, strokes which were more usually strangled at birth by the tangled long grass surrounding the village pitches. Possibly the same theory could apply to both Ralph and Jim – but to a much lesser degree.

Thus there begins an innings which is to live in the memories of all participants, an innings that in both the collective team sense and individually is so extraordinary that no story-teller would consider its invention. Fortunately, the actual score book, yellowing with age, with all the details, is still in existence.

A stunned silence fell upon the Shappley camp by the pavilion when, off the very first ball, the schoolmaster pushes a simple full-toss straight back into the Bowler's hands. What the poor chap must be feeling as he walks back no one but he will know because he gives no sign of inner turmoil – meeting the commiserations of his team-mates with his usual toothy smile, remarking wryly: "They say there's one born every minute!"

Although Ralph had done little of note with the bat in recent weeks, circumstances of the day find him at number 3. Indeed, so decimated is the team that even Jim is promoted to Number 7. Somewhat fortuitously a single comes from Ralph's bat followed by a further inexplicable tragedy when Phil Todd, the other opener, also commits batting suicide by prodding a half-volley back to the same pair of eager hands! Two opening batsmen out in the first over – both caught and bowled!

"P'raps 'es wun o' these ipponists", said the irrepressible George, "Wun o' them there whatchamacall'its what look yew in the eye an' make yew dew anything they wornt".

Ralph sees the next over through well enough – accepting four runs off a long-hop outside the off-stump which he cuts past point with obvious relish. The university coached young Squire has watched this from the non-striker's end and now faces up to the C & B expert who, with his tail up, bowls with considerable vigour, the batsman survives four deliveries – takes a rather streaky boundary to fine leg off the fifth and is clean bowled by the sixth, a torrid innings indeed. Three down now for a mere Nine Runs, leaving only four recognised run-makers available and all of them bearing the name 'Bates'. Jack comes to the wicket next – a comforting sight for the Shappley folk because he has enjoyed a good season, so far, with the bat – several twenties, a thirty-odd and even once into the forties; but not today, after an uncomfortable over or two – he, too, falls to the opening Bowler by using his pad instead of his bat to stop a straight one. Meanwhile Ralph has sneaked one or two more so it is now

Thirteen for Four Wickets with the Demon Bowler on Four for Five on a good batting pitch and a dry fast outfield! Now comes George's chance to pull things together but, alas, his leg stump becomes airborne from his second ball: "Wot 'appened then George?" asks one of the depressed gathering on his return to the fold – "Fust wun went by me ear'ole" he replies, "And the second wun I never see at all! I'm sure 'e eent tuckin' 'em down there nun!" (which, translated, means 'He's bowling very fast'). So the rather handsome scoreboard reads – HOME   TEAM: 36 ALL OUT: VISITORS 15 FOR 5 WKTS.

As Jim's moment of truth arrives, with Ralph waiting out there on ten and dinner-time imminent, he nervously asks for Middle and Leg with the Captain's words still clear in his mind – "Just stick your bat there until lunch", Mr White had requested and that is exactly what the young Number Seven does – allowing them all to troop off five minutes later with the score on 19 FOR 5 – R. BATES 16 NOT OUT JIM BATES 2 NOT OUT

Whilst the players and friends dive into their various packages and parcels and discuss the many wonders of the day so far – George, never quiet for more than two minutes, comments to his Captain that: "They tew ole boys as done well so far cent thoy?, yearse, they 'ev, done well them tew yung 'uns".

"Don't know as what we shan't beat 'em on fust innin's yll", offered Phil Todd, a forecast which everyone else considers wildly optimistic – bearing in mind the long tail that remained.

Jim kept his pad on during the interval to ensure that all would recognise his importance as a not out batsman who had not only been out there under fire and survived three hostile overs but was prepared to go again. In fact he decides to see if another pad is available because he'd already suffered one painful blow on his unprotected right shin. Batting gloves had now become acceptable and there were usually two pairs in the bag for those who chose to wear them – indeed, the Club kit had noticeably improved since the ubiquitous Schoolmaster had taken over, almost completely, the welfare and running of the Club.

Jim's inner struggle to control his excitement at the prospect and opportunity now before him, make his jam sandwiches difficult to swallow.

"Well", says Old Joe at last, "Better make another start I spect". The reply by Herbert, his London counterpart, is quite unintelligible but, as it sounds generally agreeable and is accompanied by a definite move from the horizontal to the perpendicular – Joe also struggles to his feet. The two young batsmen must wait just a *little* longer, however, because Joe has yet to refill his pipe from a worn, bulbous, tobacco pouch; a long but, obviously, enjoyable ritual. Herbert filches, from somewhere beneath his white foreman's coat, a battered tin of 'Makings' and with quite maddening deliberation proceeds to manufacture a thin-looking 'fag'.

It is nearly half past two when the match eventually restarts and young Jim has, long since, wished he'd removed his pads to ease his sweating legs. He considers asking the young Squire if it would be 'Proper' to ask for guard again on resuming his innings – but decides against it on the strength of the adage often quoted by Bill Miller, in the past, that – "It is better to remain silent and *appear* ignorant than to open your mouth and remove all doubt".

Much to everybody's surprise, especially the two youthful individuals most concerned, runs come quite comfortably when the game gets moving again. Perhaps the pitch has deadened. The Home side's total is passed and, from then on, the two upstarts fairly *gorge* themselves like starlings following the plough! Club records fall one after another. Jim passes his previous personal best of 28. A burst of applause welcomes Ralph's first ever 50. The three figure total which, before the match started, had been mooted as a possibility – then, at 15 FOR 5, hurriedly dismissed as 'Pie In The Sky' – is greeted with another show of delight from the Shappley contingent. The bowlers toil in the hot afternoon sun, they change ends, bowl *over* the wicket and *round* the wicket. The hundred partnership comes up and is followed immediately by the most marvellous moment of Jim's short cricket career when he tickles one round the corner for a single and hears another round of applause acknowledging his Half-Century.

The fast man is back on again for his third spell and produces one that knocks Jim's stumps all over the place – thus ending a stand of One Hundred and Twenty Nine – taking the total, now, to 144 FOR 6.

There is now much excited speculation as to whether Ralph might shatter all known records by making a hundred runs from his own bat, he now dominates the game – with the opposition apparently quite powerless to curb his plundering – let alone get him out! His Century duly arrives amidst much acclaim, from both sides and even some interest from players on adjoining pitches who obviously realise what is going on.

The feast is not yet over, with the stubborn resistance of the remaining make-up batsmen – Ralph carves his way to a personal One Hundred and Sixty Five Not Out – taking the team total to a monumental 268 for 9 – at which point the delighted Mr White mercifully declares the innings Closed.

Naturally, everything that follows becomes mundane – the Londoners complete their second innings, after a brief tea-interval, but, being in such a shell-shocked state, fail by over a hundred runs to match Shappley's colossal score.

Young Jim, whose feet are still, it seems, not touching the ground, views all this from his lofty mental perch with a certain amount of detachment – most of his attention being taken up with the figure '57' which, in his mind's eye, appears everywhere he looks. After all, it *was* more runs scored in one innings than he had gathered in about thirty previous opportunities, and over several seasons. Consequently, the rest of the day became very much of a blur – there was another meal somewhere, in a restaurant. Scantily-clad ladies on a stage (which he subsequently learned was the 'Golders Green Empire') and lots of getting on and off the charabanc but, in general, he was like a man who has over imbibed and retains only a vague memory of events.

No doubt, Ralph was in a similar, or even greater, state of euphoria and, in *his* case, the initial impact of his extraordinary achievement was to be extended through the interest of certain London newspapers.

CHAPTER TWENTY-SIX

Hitler Interferes

Once again outside influences were to change Jim's struggle to become a run-maker of note; this time the circumstance proved more disruptive and far-reaching than anyone could possibly have imagined. The Munich meeting between Chamberlain and Hitler had come and gone – to be followed by 'National Conscription' in preparation for possible war with Germany for the second time.

The first age group, for young men, to come under the hammer involved all those born in 1919 – a group that included Jim Bates exactly. He was not terribly concerned about the tremendous upheaval this six months training in the armed forces would cause to his domestic and working life, but what would happen to his cricket career? It was possible, of course, that the call might come in the autumn so that he would miss only a relatively unimportant football season and be back home again in time for the 1940 summer .

With these big and unsettling questions on his mind, he found it difficult to concentrate properly on anything that summer – even his batting suffered from his feeling of being in some kind of 'limbo' awaiting the wind of fate to blow him in some unknown direction into some completely-unknown life.

A couple of his ex-school mates of the same age, had already been whisked away to far distant parts of the country – as if to prove that this thing really was happening and his turn may come any day. So, try as he might, the runs failed to materialise in any worthwhile numbers – just enough to justify his position near the top of the batting order – with a DOZEN here and FIFTEEN there.

As the ominous summer moved on there came another and far greater question mark against the future; by the end of July it began to look likely that all the optimistic politicians and other pundits were going to be proved wrong and Hitler was, indeed, bent on trouble which might well affect and involve the British Empire once again. Sure enough, on that fateful Sunday morning of September Third – as Jim stood in the Village Hall porch with the other men, sheltering from the rain, the momentous news came through by wireless …

"CONSEQUENTLY WE ARE NOW AT WAR WITH GERMANY".

Somewhat selfishly perhaps, Jim's first thoughts were: 'What will happen now to the six months contract. Will I still get back to normal life and cricket again by next summer?'

He continued to exist in this strange 'in-between' state for a further six weeks or so when eventually the buff envelope bearing 'O.H.M.S.' finally arrived. Quite by chance the circumstances were, perhaps, a little odd – the climate was much different, in those days, with the season being more sharply defined. Winters seemed ever anxious to begin and left little room for Autumn; by early November freezing fogs and rime frosts took over – closely followed by the first deep snows. On this particular day Jim was working with a gang of shovel-men slowly hacking their way through many feet of snow to clear the all-important road to Town, seven miles distant. For three days solid, so far, the fifteen men had been cutting a passage through the drifts and had still progressed no more than one and a half miles from Clome, so Jim was able to pedal swiftly home each dinner time to inspect the mantlepiece – and, THERE IT WAS! propped up behind the tea-tin – 'You are required to report to H.M.S. SO-AND-SO on such and such day at 0900 hours'.

In his excitement and bewilderment his first ridiculous thought was 'I wonder if bell-bottoms are kept up with braces or with a belt?', and 'Whether I'll be sea-sick all the time or only at the beginning?' His imagination became quite incapable of building a picture of what may lie ahead. He'd never ever *seen* a warship, of course, let alone set foot on one. Whilst he re-read the instructions a second time Mrs Bates bent lower over her mixing bowl and made no answer to his garbled questions and excited comments.

He raced back to the snow-shovellers where they sat around a big log fire finishing their midday vitals – so bemused was he that his front wheel crashed straight into the burning logs before he could brake sufficiently – spewing sparks and embers over the startled diners. Their angry snarls of annoyance were quickly stifled, however, at the sight of the buff envelope in young Jim's hand – they knew well enough what it meant and were soon offering condolences – tinged, here and there perhaps by some, with a touch of envy.

Jim with his fiancee Marjorie on the day they were engaged, pictured here with his mother. Jim and Marjorie married in 1943.

CARTOON CAPTIONS

1. *Dead Bat*. 2. *Bowling Unchanged*. 3. *First Slip*. 4. *Hooking A Bumper*. 5. *Straight Drive*. 6. *Extra Cover*. 7. *Square-Leg Umpire*. 8. *Opening Bat*. 9. *Short Third Man*. 10. *Left-Arm Round*.